THE CRAFT OF FICTION

OTHER BOOKS BY PERCY LUBBOCK

Samuel Pepys

Shades of Eton

Portrait of Edith Wharton

The Percy Lubbock Reader

The
CRAFT OF FICTION

By

PERCY LUBBOCK

New York
THE VIKING PRESS

VIKING COMPASS EDITION

FOREWORD COPYRIGHT © 1957 BY THE VIKING PRESS, INC.

ALL RIGHTS RESERVED

VIKING COMPASS EDITION

ISSUED 1957 BY THE VIKING PRESS, INC.

TWELFTH PRINTING MAY 1976

SBN 670-00031-0

THIS EDITION PUBLISHED BY ARRANGEMENT WITH

JONATHAN CAPE, LTD., LONDON

LIBRARY OF CONGRESS CATALOG CARD NUMBER: 57-3468

LITHOGRAPHED IN U.S.A. BY MURRAY PRINTING CO.

FOREWORD
TO COMPASS EDITION

The Craft of Fiction was published in 1921. Six years later
E. M. Forster published *Aspects of the Novel*, and, dispelling
the apathy that had prevailed among reviewers, he recognized both the particular value of Percy Lubbock's book and
its difference from his own. "Those who follow him will lay
a sure foundation for the aesthetics of fiction," he wrote,
and, with his engagingly tyrannical gift of self-depreciation,
described his own work as "a ramshackly survey" interested
not in formal problems but in "the power of the writer to
bounce the reader into accepting what he says." If there is
one novelist in this century to whom the word "bounce" is
less applicable than it is to Mr. Forster, it is Percy Lubbock.
Except for his own great craft in fiction, Mr. Forster could
not have led us so deeply into the illusion of experience that
he creates and in which, he persuades us, we live. That is the
art of fiction.

Percy Lubbock's book was probably the first that tried to
treat fiction as an art. The editor of Henry James's letters
and of the final volumes of the New York edition of James's
novels, Lubbock performed the great service of compressing
into the small compass of *The Craft of Fiction*, and of making coherent there, those major concerns of James that per-
tained to craftsmanship, to the means that permit the novelist
to deal with his material at all. More Jamesian than James, he
was perhaps less comfortable with a novel like *War and
Peace*, which would not submit to a merely formalistic un-

FOREWORD

.derstanding, than James himself; inversely, he was even happier with *Madame Bovary*. Had he been able to go one step higher on the critical stair than his abstraction from James's technical concerns permitted him to do, he would have been able to tell us why *War and Peace* is a great work of art (still within the terms of craftsmanship) and why *Madame Bovary*, leaving James uneasy even as it becomes the *opus classicus*, is a smaller work. E. M. Forster is not Tolstoy, but his preference for dealing with "aspects" rather than with "*the* craft" of the novel indicates an important difference between the creative and the critical intelligence.

After which one must immediately say that few critics have so nearly entered the creative intelligence (even the alien creative intelligence) as Percy Lubbock. What the creative intelligence approaches by intuition, he defined in analysis. Without Lubbock's respect for the artist in the novelist, the loose form of the novel would have floundered on for how many more years without the prestige that, as a form of art, it had always deserved? He gave the criticism of the novel not only terms by means of which it could begin to discuss the question of how novels are made ("the only question I shall ask"), but also a model of the way that the question might plausibly be put. If he did not cover all its "aspects," he yet asked the primary question for criticism. And if, thirty years later, our best critics of the novel stand a step higher than he, his head is among the very few that comprise the step on which they stand.

MARK SCHORER

Berkeley, California
June 1, 1957

PREFACE
TO CURRENT EDITION

I CLAIM for this book, written more than thirty years ago, a happy title and since the title is all that I can now read of the book I incline to dwell upon its happiness The craft of fiction, not the art : they may be one and the same, the art and the craft, with no true working distinction to be drawn between them, and so indeed they are— but how differently they sound ! Art is a winged word, neither to hold nor to bind, ever ready to fly away with a discussion that would fasten it to its own ground and to the work that bears its name. The homely note of the craft allows no such distractions ; it holds you fast to the matter in hand, to the thing that has been made and the manner of its making ; nor lets you forget that the whole of the matter is contained within the finished form of the thing, and that the form was fashioned by the craft. It is like Juliet's wanton, ever ready to twitch back the escaping bird, the bird of the loftier name, with its inveterate impulse to soar from its own sphere—from the novelist's picture of life to life itself, from the world as he saw it to the world you see for your-self, and so to the rightness or wrongness of his ideas, the soundness or frailty of his opinions, the charm or disgrace of his nature. At such a height the airy discussion may all too easily range, were it not for the pluck of the string that tethers it to the thing in hand, the novel itself within its covers. Here and here only the novelist is to be watched at his work, the work by which alone he asks, and properly asks, to be judged. To watch a craftsman who knows what he is about, or to watch another who knows without knowing that he knows, which is the more absorbing ? To learn from the first is the easier learning, no doubt, if you wish to study the craft and its lore. Clear to be seen is the steady and deliberate movement of the master's hand ; and attention may be narrowed upon the gradual emergence of the form, more like sculpture indeed than picture, that stands out free and complete when the hand refrains and is withdrawn. Or is there more still to be learned from the other kind, far more largely dominant in the story of the novel—from the novelist of the liberal hand, who leaves its ruling to the free will of his genius ?—for the ruling that was implicit in his genius, if it is harder to extract, may be the broader and more embracive in its scope. It is anyhow a long day's work, with the interest of discovery in every hour of it ; and if to call it by one name rather than another is to simplify and clarify the quest, the little trick may be approved.

Moreover it is when the novel is seen in the process of its making that the dignity of the craft, if ever it was questioned, is fully restored to it. For the craft is on its honour to deal wisely and

PREFACE

faithfully with the matter entrusted to it, and to do all that is possible for its advantage. And since the matter is as various as life itself, from which it is drawn—and more still as various as the mind and temper of the novelist, whoever he is, playing upon life as he sees it—it follows that the craft must have all the versatility that is needed to meet its engagement. General principles of universal application are all very well ; but the book to be written is a particular case ; and it is indeed a simple little book if it submits to the treatment of generalities, and asks for no more. It is precisely the demands that are its very own which are of interest to the craft, as a challenge to its resourceful skill. Here is unlimited scope for the inventive imagination it is bound to display in the cause of the book that is to be ; and so the craft steps into its rank, and takes the title that belongs to it, and has no call to be shy of it, that of an art—for the lowly minister is a creator after all—without a check upon the freedom of its operations. But then again, if the craft, now safely to be called the art, is to find the means for right illustration of an idea—the idea, perhaps the wealth of ideas, which the book is to embody —yet another function accrues to it, and another dignity ; for how can it create the form till it has tested and appraised the thing that is to live in it for evermore ? But this is criticism, with yet another portion of unfettered freedom for the art, by this time entirely at ease in the name. For the art, bound though it is to treat the idea, affluent

PREFACE

or otherwise, to the best effect, can only do so if it is tractable ; and if it is a nebulous or inchoate idea that is offered it what then ?—clearly it is within the province of the art to grasp the cloud, to track the implications, in short to certify the force, the worth, the validity of the charge that is laid on it, for to these and these only it owes allegiance. Is there no such residue to be found, nor anything that finally resists the clutch of judgment ? If so, the art's responsibility is fulfilled, and it must look elsewhere for better fortunes. Enough, the honour of the craft, now as proud a name as any other, is vindicated to the full. It should not surprise us. Whenever hand and thought, working together, claim for the fruit of their partnership the value of an aesthetic satisfaction, where is criticism at last, and where creation ? Back then to the finished work, the novel within its cover : and there they are, the pair of them, commingled, for better or worse, in a natural and incessant interaction.

There is no need in these days to point to the only begetter of all our studies in this manner of approach to the novelist at work. Others no doubt, though few and soon named, had opened the way but the novel in its wayward exuberance had hardly been held to any serious account of its practice till it was called to confront the most magisterial of its makers. Henry James took the whole of its conduct in hand with a large assurance that cleared the air of certain old and obstinate misunderstandings, if only by loftily ignoring them. So massive an attention bent on a thing so familiar—the novel that everyone reads, the story that everyone can enjoy, the book of all books the least hedged from profane opinion—this was a sight (I speak with feeling) to impress, not to say spell-bind, a tentative student or an innocent reviewer of fiction. In the field of such an influence, as serene as it was great, as broad as it was bland, there was no mistaking the rawness or the thinness of a judgment mainly relying, when you came to think of it, on the two principles of " I like you, I bless you " and " I like you not, I damn you ", and there an end. If you ask Henry James whether he " likes " some book under discussion, the roll and twinkle of his eye at the simplicity of the question is a lesson in itself, and one that a young critic will never forget. Where, he seems to say, on the loose fabric of a mere preference or distaste will be found the marks of the long wear and tear of discrimination that are the true critic's honourable and recognizable warrant ? It needs a solider consistency to stand the pressure and take the imprint of the accumulating weight of his scrutiny ; and certainly there was no light fondness or hasty petulance in Henry James's praise or blame of a book. A large unhurried mind, solitarily working and never ceasing to work, entirely indifferent to the changes and chances of the popular cry, it was this that gave its sonorous gravity to Henry James's opinion of the thing that he rated, when all was said, to be the vessel of the essence of

PREFACE

life—a book. The privilege of the picture-maker, transmuting life into art, gross fact into elemental truth, was a gift in his hand of a value that alone perhaps among all others was absolute and beyond a question. And though appreciation may be as thorough as you please without the sacred gift to guide it, there is no doubt that the possession of it quickens the critic's eye for the detection of the writer at work, for catching him in the act, always supposing that he has watched his own practice as narrowly as any other. Anyhow there he stands, foursquare to all our theories of the novelist's art ; and they may blow where they list, but it is still with the burly figure of Henry James that they have first to reckon.

PERCY LUBBOCK

Lerici. 1954

THE CRAFT OF FICTION

I

To grasp the shadowy and fantasmal form of a book, to hold it fast, to turn it over and survey it at leisure—that is the effort of a critic of books, and it is perpetually defeated. Nothing, no power, will keep a book steady and motionless before us, so that we may have time to examine its shape and design. As quickly as we read, it melts and shifts in the memory; even at the moment when the last page is turned, a great part of the book, its finer detail, is already vague and doubtful. A little later, after a few days or months, how much is really left of it? A cluster of impressions, some clear points emerging from a mist of uncertainty, this is all we can hope to possess, generally speaking, in the name of a book. The experience of reading it has left something behind, and these relics we call by the book's name; but how can they be considered to give us the material for judging and appraising the book? Nobody would venture to criticize a building, a statue, a picture, with nothing before him but the memory of a single glimpse caught in passing;

I

yet the critic of literature, on the whole, has to
found his opinion upon little more. Sometimes it
is possible to return to the book and renew the
impression; to a few books we may come back
again and again, till they do in the end become
familiar sights. But of the hundreds and hundreds
of books that a critic would wish to range in his
memory, in order to scrutinize and compare them
reflectively, how many can he expect to bring
into a state of reasonable stability? Few indeed,
at the best; as for the others, he must be content
with the shapeless, incoherent visions that
respond when the recollection of them is invoked.

It is scarcely to be wondered at if criticism is
not very precise, not very exact in the use of its
terms, when it has to work at such a disadvantage.
Since we can never speak of a book with our eye
on the object, never handle a book—the real
book, which is to the volume as the symphony
to the score—our phrases find nothing to check
them, immediately and unmistakably, while they
are formed. Of a novel, for instance, that I seem
to know well, that I recall as an old acquaintance,
I may confidently begin to express an opinion;
but when, having expressed it, I would glance at
the book once more, to be satisfied that my judgement fits it, I can only turn to the image, such
as it is, that remains in a deceiving memory. The
volume lies before me, no doubt, and if it is
merely a question of detail, a name or a scene, I
can find the page and verify my sentence. But
I cannot catch a momentary sight of the book,

the book itself; I cannot look up from my writing and sharpen my impression with a straight, unhampered view of the author's work; to glance at a book, though the phrase is so often in our mouths, is in fact an impossibility. The form of a novel—and how often a critic uses that expression too—is something that none of us, perhaps, has ever really contemplated. It is revealed little by little, page by page, and it is withdrawn as fast as it is revealed; as a whole, complete and perfect, it could only exist in a more tenacious memory than most of us have to rely on. Our critical faculty may be admirable; we may be thoroughly capable of judging a book justly, if only we could watch it at ease. But fine taste and keen perception are of no use to us if we cannot retain the image of the book; and the image escapes and evades us like a cloud.

We are so well accustomed to this disability that I may seem to make too much of it. In theory, certainly, the book is never present in the critic's mind, never there in all its completeness; but enough of it, in a commonly good memory, remains to be discussed and criticized— the book as we remember it, the book that survives, is sufficient for practical purposes. Such we assume to be the case, and our criticism is very little troubled by the thought that it is only directed at certain fragments of the book which the author wrote, the rest of it having ceased to exist for us. There is plenty to say of a book, even in this condition; for the hours of our actual

THE CRAFT OF FICTION

exposure to it were full and eventful, and after living for a time with people like Clarissa Harlowe or Anna Karenina or Emma Bovary we have had a lasting experience, though the novels in which they figured may fall away into dimness and uncertainty. These women, with some of the scenes and episodes of their history, remain with us as vividly as though we had known them in life; and we still keep a general impression of their setting and their fortunes, a background more or less undefined, but associated with the thought of them. It all makes a very real and solid possession of a kind, and we readily accept it as the book itself. One does not need to remember the smaller detail of the story to perceive the truth and force of the characters; and if a great deal is forgotten, the most striking aspects of the case will linger in the mind as we look back. Dramatic episodes, fine pieces of description, above all the presence of many interesting and remarkable people—while there is so much that instantly springs to light when the book is mentioned, it seems perverse to say that the book is not before us as we write of it. The real heart and substance of the book, it might even be urged, stands out the more clearly for the obscurity into which the less essential parts of it subside.

And true it is that for criticism of the author's genius, of the power and quality of his imagination, the impressions we are able to save from oblivion are material in plenty. Of Richardson

4

and Tolstoy and Flaubert we can say at once that their command of life, their grasp of character, their knowledge of human affections and manners, had a certain range and strength and depth; we can penetrate their minds and detect the ideas that ruled there. To have lived with their creations is to have lived with them as well; with so many hours of familiar intercourse behind us we have learnt to know them, and it matters little that at any particular moment our vision of their work is bound to be imperfect. The forgotten detail has all contributed to our sense of the genius which built up and elaborated the structure, and that sense abides. Clarissa and Anna and Emma are positive facts, and so are their authors; the criticism of fiction is securely founded upon its object, if by fiction we mean something more, something other, than the novel itself—if we mean its life-like effects, and the imaginative gifts which they imply in the novelist. These we can examine as long and as closely as we choose, for they persist and grow more definite as we cultivate the remembrance of them. And to these, accordingly, we find our criticism always tending; we discuss the writer, we discuss the people in his book, we discuss the kind of life he renders and his success in the rendering. But meanwhile the book, the thing he made, lies imprisoned in the volume, and our glimpse of it was too fleeting, it seems, to leave us with a lasting knowledge of its form. We soon reach the end of so much as we have to say on that subject.

Perhaps we should have more to say of it if we read the book differently in the first place. I scarcely think we could any of us claim that in reading a novel we deliberately watch the book itself, rather than the scenes and figures it suggests, or that we seek to construct an image of the book, page by page, while its form is gradually exposed to us. We are much more inclined to forget, if we can, that the book is an object of art, and to treat it as a piece of the life around us; we fashion for ourselves, we objectify, the elements in it that happen to strike us most keenly, such as an effective scene or a brilliant character. These things take shape in the mind of the reader; they are re-created and set up where the mind's eye can rest on them. They become works of art, no doubt, in their way, but they are not the book which the author offers us. That is a larger and more complex form, one that it is much more difficult to think of as a rounded thing. A novel, as we say, opens a new world to the imagination; and it is pleasant to discover that sometimes, in a few novels, it is a world which " creates an illusion "—so pleasant that we are content to be lost in it. When that happens there is no chance of our finding, perceiving, re-creating, the form of the book. So far from losing ourselves in the world of the novel, we must hold it away from us, see it all in detachment, and use the whole of it to make the image we seek, the book itself.

It is difficult to treat a large and stirring piece

of fiction in this way. The landscape opens out and surrounds us, and we proceed to create what is in effect a novel within the novel which the author wrote. When, for example, I try to consider closely the remnant that exists in my memory of a book read and admired years ago—of such a book as Clarissa Harlowe—I well understand that in reading it I was unconsciously making a selection of my own, choosing a little of the story here and there, to form a durable image, and that my selection only included such things as I could easily work into shape. The girl herself, first of all—if she, though so much of her story has faded away, is still visibly present, it is because nothing is simpler than to create for oneself the idea of a human being, a figure and a character, from a series of glimpses and anecdotes. Creation of this kind we practise every day; we are continually piecing together our fragmentary evidence about the people around us and moulding their images in thought. It is the way in which we make our world; partially, imperfectly, very much at haphazard, but still perpetually, everybody deals with his experience like an artist. And his talent, such as it may be, for rounding and detaching his experience of a man or a woman, so that the thing stands clear in his thought and takes the light on every side—this can never lie idle, it is exercised every hour of the day.

As soon as he begins to hear of Clarissa, therefore, on the first page of Richardson's book, the shaping, objectifying mind of the reader is at work on familiar material. It is so easy to construct the idea of the exquisite creature, that she seems to step from the pages of her own accord; I, as I read, am aware of nothing but that a new acquaintance is gradually becoming better and better known to me. No conscious effort is needed to make a recognizable woman of her, though in fact I am fitting a multitude of small details together, as I proceed to give her the body and mind that she presently possesses. And so, too, with the lesser people in the book, and with their surroundings; so, too, with the incidents that pass; a succession of moments are visualized, are wrought into form by the reader, though perhaps very few of them are so well made that they will last in memory. If they soon disappear, the fault may be the writer's or the reader's, Richardson's if he failed to describe them adequately, mine if my manner of reading has not been sufficiently creative. In any case the page that has been well read has the best chance of survival; it was soundly fashioned, to start with, out of the material given me by the writer, and at least it will resist the treachery of a poor memory more resolutely than a page that I did not thoroughly recreate.

But still, as I say, the aspects of a book that for the most part we detach and solidify are simply those which cost us no deliberate pains. We bring to the reading of a book certain imaginative faculties which are in use all the day long, faculties that enable us to complete, in our minds, the people and the scenes which the novelist describes—to give them dimensions, to see round them, to make them " real." And these faculties, no doubt, when they are combined with a trained taste, a sense of quality, seem to represent all that is needed for the criticism of fiction. The novel (and in these pages I speak only of the modern novel, the picture of life that we are in a position to understand without the knowledge of a student or a scholar)—the modern novel asks for no other equipment in its readers than this common gift, used as instinctively as the power of breathing, by which we turn the flat impressions of our senses into solid shapes: this gift, and nothing else except that other, certainly much less common, by which we discriminate between the thing that is good of its kind and the thing that is bad. Such, I should think, is very nearly the theory of our criticism in the matter of the art of fiction. A novel is a picture of life, and life is well known to us; let us first of all " realize " it, and then, using our taste, let us judge whether it is true, vivid, convincing—like life, in fact.

The theory does indeed go a little further, we know. A novel is a picture, a portrait, and we do not forget that there is more in a portrait than the " likeness." Form, design, composition, are to be sought in a novel, as in any other work of art; a novel is the better for possessing them. That we must own, if fiction is an art at all; and

9

an art it must be, since a literal transcript of life is plainly impossible. The laws of art, therefore, apply to this object of our scrutiny, this novel, and it is the better, other things being equal, for obeying them. And yet, is it so very much the better? Is it not somehow true that fiction, among the arts, is a peculiar case, unusually exempt from the rules that bind the rest? Does the fact that a novel is well designed, well proportioned, really make a very great difference in its power to please?—and let us answer honestly, for if it does not, then it is pedantry to force these rules upon a novel. In other arts it may be otherwise, and no doubt a lop-sided statue or an ill-composed painting is a plain offence to the eye, however skilfully it may copy life. The same thing is true of a novel, perhaps, if the fault is very bad, very marked; yet it would be hard to say that even so it is necessarily fatal, or that a novel cannot triumphantly live down the worst aberrations of this kind. We know of novels which everybody admits to be badly constructed, but which are so full of life that it does not appear to matter. May we not conclude that form, design, composition, have a rather different bearing upon the art of fiction than any they may have elsewhere?

And, moreover, these expressions, applied to the viewless art of literature, must fit it loosely and insecurely at best—does it not seem so? They are words usurped from other arts, words that suppose a visible and measurable object, painted or carved. For criticizing the craft of fiction we have no other language than that which has been devised for the material arts; and though we may feel that to talk of the colours and values and perspective of a novel is natural and legitimate, yet these are only metaphors, after all, that cannot be closely pressed. A book starts a train of ideas in the head of the reader, ideas which are massed and arranged on some kind of system; but it is only by the help of fanciful analogies that we can treat the mass as a definite object. Such phrases may give hints and suggestions concerning the method of the novelist; the whole affair is too nebulous for more. Even if a critic's memory were infallible, as it can never be, still it would be impossible for him to give a really scientific account of the structure of the simplest book, since in the last resort he cannot lay his finger upon a single one of the effects to which he refers. When two men stand looking at a picture, at least their two lines of vision meet at a point upon the canvas; they may dispute about it, but the picture stands still. And even then they find that criticism has its difficulties, it would appear. The literary critic, with nothing to point to but the mere volume in his hand, must recognize that his wish to be precise, to be definite, to be clear and exact in his statements, is hopelessly vain.

It is all undeniable, no doubt; from every side we make out that the criticism of a book—not the people in the book, not the character of the author, but the book—is impossible. We cannot remember the book, and even if we could, we should still be unable to describe it in literal and unequivocal terms. It cannot be done; and the only thing to be said is that perhaps it can be approached, perhaps the book can be seen, a little more closely in one way than in another. It is a modest claim, and my own attempt to assert it will be still more modest. A few familiar novels, possibly a dozen, by still fewer writers— it will be enough if I can view this small handful with some particularity. And I shall consider them, too, with no idea of criticizing all their aspects, or even more than one. How they are made is the only question I shall ask; and though indeed that is a question which incidentally raises a good many others—questions of the intention of the novelist, his choice of a subject, the manner of his imagination, and so forth—these I shall follow no further than I can help. And as for the few novels that I shall speak of, they will be such as appear to illustrate most plainly the various elements of the craft; one need not range widely to find them, nor does it matter if the selection, from any other point of view, should seem arbitrary. Many great names may be passed over, for it is not always the greatest whose method of work gives the convenient example; on the other hand the best example is always to be found among the great, and it is essential to keep to their company.

But something may first be said of the reading

of a novel. The beginning of criticism is to read aright, in other words to get into touch with the book as nearly as may be. It is a forlorn enterprise—that is admitted; but there are degrees of unsuccess.

II

A BOOK has a certain form, we all agree; what the form of a particular book may be, whether good or bad, and whether it matters—these are points of debate; but that a book *has* a form, this is not disputed. We hear the phrase on all sides, an unending argument is waged over it. One critic condemns a novel as " shapeless," meaning that its shape is objectionable; another retorts that if the novel has other fine qualities, its shape is unimportant; and the two will continue their controversy till an onlooker, pardonably bewildered, may begin to suppose that " form " in fiction is something to be put in or left out of a novel according to the taste of the author. But though the discussion is indeed confusingly worded at times, it is clear that there is agreement on this article at least—that a book is a thing to which a shape is ascribable, good or bad. I have spoken of the difficulty that prevents us from ever seeing or describing the shape with perfect certainty; but evidently we are convinced that it is there, clothing the book.

Not as a single form, however, but as a moving stream of impressions, paid out of the volume in a slender thread as we turn the pages—that is how the book reaches us; or in another image it is a procession that passes before us as we sit to watch. It is hard to think of this lapse and flow, this sequence of figures and scenes, which must be taken in a settled order, one after another, as existing in the condition of an immobile form, like a pile of sculpture. Though we readily talk of the book as a material work of art, our words seem to be crossed by a sense that it is rather a process, a passage of experience, than a thing of size and shape. I find this contradiction dividing all my thought about books; they are objects, yes, completed and detached, but I recall them also as tracts of time, during which Clarissa and Anna moved and lived and endured in my view. Criticism is hampered by the ambiguity; the two books, the two aspects of the same book, blur each other; a critic seems to shift from this one to that, from the thing carved in the stuff of thought to the passing movement of life. And on the whole it is the latter aspect of the two which asserts itself; the first, the novel with its formal outline, appears for a moment, and then the life contained in it breaks out and obscures it.

But the procession which passes across our line of sight in the reading must be marshalled and concentrated somewhere; we receive the story of Anna bit by bit, all the numerous fragments that together make Tolstoy's book; and finally the tale is complete, and the book stands before us, or should stand, as a welded mass. We have been given the material, and the book should now be there. Our treacherous memory will have failed to preserve it all, but that disability we have admitted and discounted; at any rate an imposing object ought to remain, Tolstoy's great imaginative sculpture, sufficiently representing his intention. And again and again, at this point, I make the same discovery; I have been watching the story, that is to say, forgetful of the fact that there was more for me to do than to watch receptively and passively, forgetful of the novel that I should have been fashioning out of the march of experience as it passed. I have been treating it as life; and that is all very well, and is the right manner as far as it goes, but my treatment of life is capricious and eclectic, and this life, this story of Anna, has suffered accordingly. I have taken much out of it and carried away many recollections; I have omitted to think of it as matter to be wrought into a single form. What wonder if I search my mind in vain, a little later, for the book that Tolstoy wrote?

But how is one to construct a novel out of the impressions that Tolstoy pours forth from his prodigious hands? This is a kind of " creative reading " (the phrase is Emerson's) which comes instinctively to few of us. We know how to imagine a landscape or a conversation when he describes it, but to gather up all these sights and sounds into a compact fabric, round which the mind can wander freely, as freely as it strays and contemplates and loses its way, perhaps, in Tolstoy's wonderful world—this is a task which does not achieve itself without design and deliberation on the part of the reader. It is an effort, first of all, to keep the world of Anna (I cling to this illustration) at a distance; and yet it must be kept at a distance if it is to be impressed with the form of art; no artist (and the skilful reader is an artist) can afford to be swayed and beset by his material, he must stand above it. And then it is a further effort, prolonged, needing practice and knowledge, to recreate the novel in its right form, the best form that the material, selected and disposed by the author, is capable of accepting.

The reader of a novel—by which I mean the critical reader—is himself a novelist; he is the maker of a book which may or may not please his taste when it is finished, but of a book for which he must take his own share of the responsibility. The author does his part, but he cannot transfer his book like a bubble into the brain of the critic; he cannot make sure that the critic will possess his work. The reader must therefore become, for his part, a novelist, never permitting himself to suppose that the creation of the book is solely the affair of the author. The difference between them is immense, of course, and so much so that a critic is always inclined to extend and intensify it. The opposition that he conceives between the creative and the critical task is a very real one; but in modestly belittling his own side of the business he is apt to forget an essential portion of it. The writer of the novel works in a manner that would be utterly impossible to the critic, no doubt, and with a liberty and with a range that would disconcert him entirely. But in one quarter their work coincides; both of them make the novel.

Is it necessary to define the difference? That is soon done if we picture Tolstoy and his critic side by side, surveying the free and formless expanse of the world of life. The critic has nothing to say; he waits, looking to Tolstoy for guidance. And Tolstoy, with the help of some secret of his own, which is his genius, does not hesitate for an instant. His hand is plunged into the scene, he lifts out of it great fragments, right and left, ragged masses of life torn from their setting; he selects. And upon these trophies he sets to work with the full force of his imagination; he detects their significance, he disengages and throws aside whatever is accidental and meaningless; he re-makes them in conditions that are never known in life, conditions in which a thing is free to grow according to its own law, expressing itself unhindered; he liberates and completes. And then, upon all this new life—so like the old and yet so different, *more* like the old, as one may say, than the old ever had the chance of being— upon all this life that is now so much more intensely living than before, Tolstoy directs the skill of his art; he distributes it in a single, embracing design; he orders and disposes. And thus the critic receives his guidance, and *his* work begins.

No selection, no arrangement is required of him; the new world that is laid before him is the world of art, life liberated from the tangle of cross-purposes, saved from arbitrary distortion. Instead of a continuous, endless scene, in which the eye is caught in a thousand directions at once, with nothing to hold it to a fixed centre, the landscape that opens before the critic is whole and single; it has passed through an imagination, it has shed its irrelevancy and is compact with its own meaning. Such is the world in the book—in Tolstoy's book I do not say; but it is the world in the book as it may be, in the book where imagination and execution are perfectly harmonized. And in any case the critic accepts this ordered, enhanced display as it stands, better or worse, and uses it all for the creation of the book. There can be no picking and choosing now; that was the business of the novelist, and it has been accomplished according to his light; the critic creates out of life that is already subject to art.

But his work is not the less plastic for that. The impressions that succeed one another, as the pages of the book are turned, are to be built into a structure, and the critic is missing his opportunity unless he can proceed in a workmanlike manner. It is not to be supposed that an artist who carves or paints is so filled with emotion by the meaning of his work—the story in it—that he forgets the abstract beauty of form and colour; and though there is more room for such sensibility in an art which is the shaping of thought and feeling, in the art of literature, still the man of letters is a craftsman, and the critic cannot be less. He must know how to handle the stuff which is continually forming in his mind while he reads; he must be able to recognize its fine variations and to take them all into account. Nobody can work in material of which the properties are unfamiliar, and a reader who tries to get possession of a book with nothing but his appreciation of the life and the ideas and the story in it is like a man who builds a wall without knowing the capacities of wood and clay and stone. Many different substances, as distinct to the practised eye as stone and wood, go to the making of a novel, and it is necessary to see them for what they are. So only is it possible to use them aright, and to find, when the volume is closed, that a complete, coherent, appraisable book remains in the mind.

And what are these different substances, and how is a mere reader to learn their right use? They are the various forms of narrative, the forms in which a story may be told; and while they are many, they are not indeed so very many, though their modifications and their commixtures are infinite. They are not recondite; we know them well and use them freely, but to use them is easier than to perceive their demands and their qualities. These we gradually discern by using them consciously and questioningly—by reading, I mean, and reading critically, the books in which they

THE CRAFT OF FICTION

appear. Let us very carefully follow the methods
of the novelists whose effects are incontestable,
noticing exactly the manner in which the scenes
and figures in their books are presented.   The
scenes and figures, as I have said, we shape, we
detach, without the smallest difficulty ; and if we
pause over them for long enough to see by what
arts and devices, on the author's part, we have
been enabled to shape them so strikingly—to see
precisely how this episode has been given relief,
that character made intelligible and vivid—we at
once begin to stumble on many discoveries about
the making of a novel.

Our criticism has been oddly incurious in the
matter, considering what the dominion of the
novel has been for a hundred and fifty years. The
refinements of the art of fiction have been accepted
without question, or at most have been classified
roughly and summarily—as is proved by the
singular poverty of our critical vocabulary, as
soon as we pass beyond the simplest and plainest
effects.   The expressions and the phrases at our
disposal bear no defined, delimited meanings ;
they have not been rounded and hardened by
passing constantly from one critic's hand to
another's.   What is to be understood by a
" dramatic " narrative, a " pictorial " narrative,
a " scenic " or a " generalized " story ? We must
use such words, as soon as we begin to examine
the structure of a novel ; and yet they are words
which have no technical acceptation in regard to
a novel, and one cannot be sure how they will be

taken. The want of a received nomenclature is a real hindrance, and I have often wished that the modern novel had been invented a hundred years sooner, so that it might have fallen into the hands of the critical schoolmen of the seventeenth century. As the production of an age of romance, or of the eve of such an age, it missed the advantage of the dry light of academic judgement, and I think it still has reason to regret the loss. The critic has, at any rate; his language, even now, is unsettled and unformed.

And we still suffer from a kind of shyness in the presence of a novel. From shyness of the author or of his sentiments or of his imagined world, no indeed; but we are haunted by a sense that a novel is a piece of life, and that to take it to pieces would be to destroy it. We begin to analyse it, and we seem to be like Beckmesser, writing down the mistakes of the spring-time upon his slate. It is an obscure delicacy, not clearly formulated, not admitted, perhaps, in so many words; but it has its share in restraining the hand of criticism. We scarcely need to be thus considerate; the immense and necessary difficulty of closing with a book at all, on any terms, might appear to be enough, without adding another; the book is safe from rude violation. And it is not a piece of life, it is a piece of art like another; and the fact that it is an ideal shape, with no existence in space, only to be spoken of in figures and metaphors, makes it all the more important that in our thought it should be protected by no romantic scruple. Or perhaps it is not really the book that we are shy of, but a still more fugitive phantom— our pleasure in it. It spoils the fun of a novel to know how it is made—is this a reflection that lurks at the back of our minds? Sometimes, I think.

But the pleasure of illusion is small beside the pleasure of creation, and the greater is open to every reader, volume in hand. How a novelist finds his subject, in a human being or in a situation or in a turn of thought, this indeed is beyond us; we might look long at the very world that Tolstoy saw, we should never detect the unwritten book he found there; and he can seldom (he and the rest of them) give any account of the process of discovery. The power that recognizes the fruitful idea and seizes it is a thing apart. For this reason we judge the novelist's eye for a subject to be his cardinal gift, and we have nothing to say, whether by way of exhortation or of warning, till his subject is announced. But from that moment he is accessible, his privilege is shared; and the delight of treating the subject is acute and perennial. From point to point we follow the writer, always looking back to the subject itself in order to understand the logic of the course he pursues. We find that we are creating a design, large or small, simple or intricate, as the chapter finished is fitted into its place; or again there is a flaw and a break in the development, the author takes a turn that appears to contradict or to disregard the subject,

THE CRAFT OF FICTION

and the critical question, strictly so called, begins.
Is this proceeding of the author the right one,
the best for the subject? Is it possible to conceive
and to name a better? The hours of the author's
labour are lived again by the reader, the pleasure
of creation is renewed.

So it goes, till the book is ended and we look
back at the whole design. It may be absolutely
satisfying to the eye, the expression of the
subject, complete and compact. But with the
book in this condition of a defined shape, firm of
outline, its form shows for what it is indeed—not
an attribute, one of many and possibly not the
most important, but the book itself, as the form
of a statue is the statue itself. If the form is to
the eye imperfect, it means that the subject is
somehow and somewhere imperfectly expressed,
it means that the story has suffered. Where
then, and how? Is it because the treatment has
not started from the heart of the subject, or has
diverged from the line of its true development—
or is it that the subject itself was poor and un-
fruitful? The question ramifies quickly. But
anyhow here is the book, or something that we
need not hesitate to regard as the book, re-
created according to the best of the reader's
ability. Indeed he knows well that it will melt
away in time; nothing can altogether save it;
only it will last for longer than it would have
lasted if it had been read uncritically, if it had
not been deliberately recreated. In that case it
would have fallen to pieces at once, Anna and

24

Clarissa would have stepped out of the work of art in which their authors had so laboriously enshrined them, the book would have perished. It is now a single form, and let us judge the effect of it while we may. At best we shall have no more time than we certainly require.

III

A GREAT and brilliant novel, a well-known novel, and at the same time a large and crowded and unmanageable novel—such will be the book to consider first. It must be one that is universally admitted to be a work of genius, signal and conspicuous; I wish to examine its form, I do not wish to argue its merit; it must be a book which it is superfluous to praise, but which it will never seem too late to praise again. It must also be well known, and this narrows the category; the novel of whose surpassing value every one is convinced may easily fall outside it; our novel must be one that is not only commended, but habitually read. And since we are concerned with the difficulty of controlling the form of a novel, let it be an evident case of the difficulty, an extreme case on a large scale, where the question cannot be disguised—a novel of ample scope, covering wide spaces and many years, long and populous and eventful. The category is reduced indeed; perhaps it contains one novel only, War and Peace.

Of War and Peace it has never been suggested, I suppose, that Tolstoy here produced a model of perfect form. It is a panoramic vision of

26

people and places, a huge expanse in which armies are marshalled; can one expect of such a book that it should be neatly composed? It is crowded with life, at whatever point we face it; intensely vivid, inexhaustibly stirring, the broad impression is made by the big prodigality of Tolstoy's invention. If a novel could really be as large as life, Tolstoy could easily fill it; his great masterful reach never seems near its limit; he is always ready to annex another and yet another tract of life, he is only restrained by the mere necessity of bringing a novel somewhere to an end. And then, too, this mighty command of spaces and masses is only half his power. He spreads further than any one else, but he also touches the detail of the scene, the single episode, the fine shade of character, with exquisite lightness and precision. Nobody surpasses, in some ways nobody approaches, the easy authority with which he handles the matter immediately before him at the moment, a roomful of people, the brilliance of youth, spring sunshine in a forest, a boy on a horse; whatever his shifting panorama brings into view, he makes of it an image of beauty and truth that is final, complete, unqualified. Before the profusion of War and Peace the question of its general form is scarcely raised. It is enough that such a world should have been pictured; it is idle to look for proportion and design in a book that contains a world.

But for this very reason, that there is so much in the book to distract attention from its form, it is particularly interesting to ask how it is made. The doubt, the obvious perplexity, is a challenge to the exploring eye. It may well be that effective composition on such a scale is impossible, but it is not so easy to say exactly where Tolstoy fails. If the total effect of his book is inconclusive, it is all lucidity and shapeliness in its parts. There is no faltering in his hold upon character; he never loses his way among the scores of men and women in the book; and in all the endless series of scenes and events there is not one which betrays a hesitating intention. The story rolls on and on, and it is long before the reader can begin to question its direction. Tolstoy *seems* to know precisely where he is going, and why; there is nothing at any moment to suggest that he is not in perfect and serene control of his idea. Only at last, perhaps, we turn back and wonder what it was. What is the subject of War and Peace, what is the novel *about*? There is no very ready answer; but if we are to discover what is wrong with the form, this is the question to press.

What is the story? There is first of all a succession of phases in the lives of certain generations; youth that passes out into maturity, fortunes that meet and clash and re-form, hopes that flourish and wane and reappear in other lives, age that sinks and hands on the torch to youth again—such is the substance of the drama. The book, I take it, begins to grow out of the thought of the processional march of the generations, always changing, always renewed; its figures are sought and chosen for the clarity with which the drama is embodied in them. Young people of different looks and talents, moods and tempers, but young with the youth of all times and places—the story is alive with them at once. The Rostov household resounds with them—the Rostovs are of the easy, light-spirited, quick-tongued sort. Then there is the dreary old Bolkonsky mansion, with Andrew, generous and sceptical, and with poor plain Marya, ardent and repressed. And for quite another kind of youth, there is Peter Besukhov, master of millions, fat and good-natured and indolent, his brain a fever of faiths and aspirations which not he, but Andrew, so much more sparing in high hopes, has the tenacity to follow. These are in the foreground, and between and behind them are more and more, young men and women at every turn, crowding forward to take their places as the new generation.

It does not matter, it does not affect the drama, that they are men and women of a certain race and century, soldiers, politicians, princes, Russians in an age of crisis; such they are, with all the circumstances of their time and place about them, but such they are in secondary fashion, it is what they happen to be. Essentially they are not princes, not Russians, but figures in the great procession; they are here in the book because they are young, not because they are the rising hope of Russia in the years of Austerlitz and Borodino. It is laid upon them primarily to enact the cycle of birth and growth, death and birth again. They illustrate the story that is the same always and everywhere, and the tumult of the dawning century to which they are born is an accident. Peter and Andrew and Natasha and the rest of them are the children of yesterday and to-day and to-morrow; there is nothing in any of them that is not of all time. Tolstoy has no thought of showing them as the children of their particular conditions, as the generation that was formed by a certain historic struggle; he sees them simply as the embodiment of youth. To an English reader of to-day it is curious—and more, it is strangely moving—to note how faithfully the creations of Tolstoy, the nineteenth-century Russian, copy the young people of the twentieth century and of England; it is all one, life in Moscow then, life in London now, provided only that it is young enough. Old age is rather more ephemeral; its period is written on it (not very deeply, after all), and here and there it " dates." Nicholas and Natasha are always of the newest modernity.

Such is the master-motive that at first sight appears to underlie the book, in spite of its name; such is the most evident aspect of the story, as our thought brushes freely and rapidly around it. In this drama the war and the peace are episodic, not of the centre; the historic scene is used as a foil and a background. It appears from time to time, for the sake of its value in throwing the nearer movement of life into strong relief; it very powerfully and strikingly shows what the young people *are*. The drama of the rise of a generation is nowhere more sharply visible and appreciable than it is in such a time of convulsion. Tolstoy's moment is well chosen; his story has a setting that is fiercely effective, the kind of setting which in our Europe this story has indeed found very regularly, century by century. But it is not by the war, from this point of view, that the multifarious scenes are linked together; it is by another idea, a more general, as we may still dare to hope, than the idea of war. Youth and age, the flow and the ebb of the recurrent tide—this is the theme of Tolstoy's book.

So it seems for a while. But Tolstoy called his novel War and Peace, and presently there arises a doubt; did he believe himself to be writing *that* story, and not the story of Youth and Age? I have been supposing that he named his book carelessly (he would not be alone among great novelists for that), and thereby emphasized the wrong side of his intention; but there are things in the drama which suggest that his title really represented the book he projected. Cutting across the big human motive I have indicated, there falls a second line of thought, and sometimes it is this, most clearly, that the author is following. Not the cycle of life everlasting, in which the rage of nations is an incident, a noise and an incursion from without—but the strife itself, the irrelevant uproar, becomes the motive of the fable. War and Peace, the drama of that ancient alternation, is now the subject out of which the form of the book is to grow. Not seldom, and more frequently as the book advances, the story takes this new and contradictory alignment. The centre shifts from the general play of life, neither national nor historic, and plants itself in the field of racial conflict, typified by that " sheep-worry of Europe " which followed the French Revolution. The young people immediately change their meaning. They are no longer there for their own sake, guardians of the torch for their hour. They are re-disposed, partially and fitfully, in another relation; they are made to figure as creatures of the Russian scene, at the impact of East and West in the Napoleonic clash.

It is a mighty antinomy indeed, on a scale adapted to Tolstoy's giant imagination. With one hand he takes up the largest subject in the world, the story to which all other human stories are subordinate; and not content with this, in the other hand he produces the drama of a great historic collision, for which a scene is set with no less prodigious a gesture. And there is not a sign in the book to show that he knew what he was doing; apparently he was quite unconscious that he was writing two novels at once. Such an over-sight is not peculiar to men of genius, I dare say; the least of us is capable of the feat, many of us are seen to practise it. But two such novels as these, two such immemorial epics, caught up together and written out in a couple of thousand pages, inadvertently mixed and entangled, and all with an air of composure never ruffled or embarrassed, in a style of luminous simplicity— it was a feat that demanded, that betokened, the genius of Tolstoy. War and Peace is like an Iliad, the story of certain men, and an Aeneid, the story of a nation, compressed into one book by a man who never so much as noticed that he was Homer and Virgil by turns.

Or can it perhaps be argued that he was aware of the task he set himself, and that he intentionally coupled his two themes? He proposed, let us say, to set the unchanging story of life against the momentary tumult, which makes such a stir in the history-books, but which passes, leaving the other story still unrolling for ever. Perhaps he did; but I am looking only at his book, and I can see no hint of it in the length and breadth of the novel as it stands; I can discover no angle at which the two stories will appear to unite and merge in a single impression. Neither is subordinate to the other, and there is nothing above them (what more *could* there be?) to which they are both related. Nor are they placed together to illustrate a contrast; nothing *results* from their juxtaposition. Only from time to time, upon no apparent principle and without a word of warning, one of them is dropped and the other resumed. It would be possible, I think, to mark the exact places—not always even at the end of a chapter, but casually, in the middle of a page—where the change occurs. The reader begins to look out for them; in the second half of the novel they are liberally sprinkled.

The long, slow, steady sweep of the story—the *first* story, as I call it—setting through the personal lives of a few young people, bringing them together, separating them, dimming their freshness, carrying them away from hopeful adventure to their appointed condition, where their part is only to transmit the gift of youth to others and to drop back while the adventure is repeated— this motive, in which the book opens and closes and to which it constantly returns, is broken into by the famous scenes of battle (by some of them, to be accurate, not by all), with the reverberation of imperial destinies, out of which Tolstoy makes a saga of his country's tempestuous past. It is magnificent, this latter, but it has no bearing on the other, the universal story of no time or country, the legend of every age, which is told of Nicholas and Natasha, but which might have been told as well of the sons and daughters of the king of Troy. To Nicholas, the youth of all time, the strife of Emperor and Czar is the occasion, it may very well be, of the climax of his adventure; but it is no more than the occasion, not essential to it, since by some means or other he would have touched his climax in any age. War and peace are likely enough to shape his life for him, whether he belongs to ancient Troy or to modern Europe; but if it is *his* story, his and that of his companions, why do we see them suddenly swept into the background, among the figures that

34

populate the story of a particular and memorable war? For that is what happens.

It is now the war, with the generals and the potentates in the forefront, that is the matter of the story. Alexander and Kutusov, Napoleon and Murat, become the chief actors, and between them the play is acted out. In this story the loves and ambitions of the young generation, which have hitherto been central, are relegated to the fringe; there are wide tracts in which they do not appear at all. Again and again Tolstoy forgets them entirely; he has discovered a fresh idea for the unification of this second book, a theory drummed into the reader with merciless iteration, desolating many a weary page. The meaning of the book—and it is extraordinary how Tolstoy's artistic sense deserts him in expounding it—lies in the relation between the man of destiny and the forces that he dreams he is directing; it is a high theme, but Tolstoy cannot leave it to make its own effect. He, whose power of making a story *tell itself* is unsurpassed, is capable of thrusting into his book interminable chapters of comment and explanation, chapters in the manner of a controversial pamphlet, lest the argument of his drama should be missed. But the reader at last takes an easy way with these maddening interruptions; wherever " the historians " are mentioned he knows that several pages can be turned at once; Tolstoy may be left to belabour the conventional theories of the Napoleonic legend and rejoined later on, when

35

it has occurred to him once more that he is writing a novel.

When he is not pamphleteering Tolstoy's treatment of the second story, the national saga, is masterly at every point. If we could forget the original promise of the book as lightly as its author does, nothing could be more impressive than his pictures of the two hugely-blundering masses, Europe and Russia, ponderously colliding at the apparent dictation of a few limited brains —so few, so limited, that the irony of their claim to be the directors of fate is written over all the scene. Napoleon at the crossing of the Niemen, Napoleon before Moscow, the Russian council of war after Borodino (gravely watched by the small child Malasha, overlooked in her corner), Kutusov, wherever he appears—all these are impressions belonging wholly to the same cycle; they have no effect in relation to the story of Peter and Nicholas, they do not extend or advance it, but on their own account they are supreme. There are not enough of them, and they are not properly grouped and composed, to *complete* the second book that has forced its way into the first; the cycle of the war and the peace, as distinguished from the cycle of youth and age, is broken and fragmentary. The size of the theme, and the scale upon which these scenes are drawn, imply a novel as long as our existing War and Peace; it would all be filled by Kutusov and Napoleon, if their drama were fully treated, leaving no room for another. But, mutilated as it is, each of the fragments is broadly handled, highly finished, and perfectly adjusted to a point of view that is not the point of view for the rest of the book.

And it is to be remarked that the lines of cleavage—which, as I suggested, can be traced with precision—by no means invariably divide the peaceful scenes of romance from the battles and intrigues of the historic struggle, leaving these on one side, those on the other. Sometimes the great public events are used as the earlier theme demands that they should be used—as the material in which the stoiy of youth is embodied. Consider, for instance, one of the earlier battle-pieces in the book, where Nicholas, very youthful indeed, is for the first time under fire; he comes and goes bewildered, laments like a lost child, is inspired with heroism and flees like a hare for his life. As Tolstoy presents it, this battle, or a large part of it, is the affair of Nicholas; it belongs to him, it is a piece of experience that enters his life and enriches our sense of it. Many of the wonderful chapters, again, which deal with the abandonment and the conflagration of Moscow, are seen through the lives of the irrepressible Rostov household, or of Peter in his squalid imprisonment; the scene is framed in their consciousness. Prince Andrew, too—nobody can forget how much of the battle in which he is mortally wounded is transformed into an emotion of *his*; those pages are filched from Tolstoy's theory of the war and given to his fiction. In all these episodes, and in others of the same kind, the history of the time is in the background; in front of it, closely watched for their own sake, are the lives which that history so deeply affects.

But in the other series of pictures of the campaign, mingled with these, it is different. They are admirable, but they screen the thought of the particular lives in which the wider interest of the book (as I take it to be) is firmly lodged. From a huge emotion that reaches us through the youth exposed to it, the war is changed into an emotion of our own. It is rendered by the story-teller, on the whole, as a scene directly faced by himself, instead of being reflected in the experience of the rising generation. It is true that Tolstoy's good instinct guides him ever and again away from the mere telling of the story on his own authority; at high moments he knows better than to tell it himself. He approaches it through the mind of an onlooker, Napoleon or Kutusov or the little girl by the stove in the corner, borrowing the value of indirectness, the increased effect of a story that is seen as it is mirrored in the mind of another. But he chooses his onlooker at random and follows no consistent method. The predominant point of view is simply his own, that of the independent story-teller; so that the general effect of these pictures is made on a totally different principle from that which governs the story of the young people. In that story— though there, too, Tolstoy's method is far from being consistent—the effect is *mainly* based on our free sharing in the hopes and fears and meditations of the chosen few. In the one case Tolstoy is immediately beside us, narrating; in the other it is Peter and Andrew, Nicholas and Natasha, who are with us and about us, and Tolstoy is effaced.

Here, then, is the reason, or at any rate one of the reasons, why the general shape of War and Peace fails to satisfy the eye—as I suppose it admittedly to fail. It is a confusion of two designs, a confusion more or less masked by Tolstoy's imperturbable ease of manner, but revealed by the look of his novel when it is seen as a whole. It has no centre, and Tolstoy is so clearly unconcerned by the lack that one must conclude he never perceived it. If he had he would surely have betrayed that he had; he would have been found, at some point or other, trying to gather his two stories into one, devising a scheme that would include them both, establishing a centre somewhere. But no, he strides through his book without any such misgiving, and really it is his assurance that gives it such an air of lucidity. He would only have flawed its surface by attempting to force the material on his hands into some sort of unity; its incongruity is fundamental. And when we add, as we must, that War and Peace, with all this, is one of the great novels of the world, a picture of life that has never been surpassed for its grandeur and its beauty, there is a moment when all our criticism perhaps seems trifling. What does it matter?

39

The business of the novelist is to create life, and here is life created indeed; the satisfaction of a clean, coherent form is wanting, and it would be well to have it, but that is all. We have a magnificent novel without it.

So we have, but we might have had a more magnificent still, and a novel that would not be *this* novel merely, this War and Peace, with the addition of another excellence, a comeliness of form. We might have had a novel that would be a finer, truer, more vivid and more forcible picture of life. The best form is that which makes the most of its subject—there is no other definition of the meaning of form in fiction. The well-made book is the book in which the subject and the form coincide and are indistinguishable—the book in which the matter is all used up in the form, in which the form expresses all the matter. Where there is disagreement and conflict between the two, there is stuff that is superfluous or there is stuff that is wanting; the form of the book, as it stands before us, has failed to do justice to the idea. In War and Peace, as it seems to me, the story suffers twice over for the imperfection of the form. It is damaged, in the first place, by the importation of another and an irrelevant story—damaged because it so loses the sharp and clear relief that it would have if it stood alone. Whether the story was to be the drama of youth and age, or the drama of war and peace, in either case it would have been incomparably more impressive if *all* the great wealth of the material had been used for its purpose, all brought into one design. And furthermore, in either case again, the story is incomplete; neither of them is finished, neither of them is given its full development, for all the size of the book. But to this point, at least in relation to one of the two, I shall return directly.

Tolstoy's novel is wasteful of its subject; that is the whole objection to its loose, unstructural form. Criticism bases its conclusion upon nothing whatever but the injury done to the story, the loss of its full potential value. Is there so much that is good in War and Peace that its inadequate grasp of a great theme is easily forgotten? It is not only easily forgotten, it is scarcely noticed— on a first reading of the book; I speak at least for one reader. But with every return to it the book that *might* have been is more insistent; it obtrudes more plainly, each time, interfering with the book that is. Each time, in fact, it becomes harder to make a book of it at all; instead of holding together more firmly, with every successive reconstruction, its prodigious members seem always more disparate and disorganized; they will not coalesce. A subject, one and whole and irreducible—a novel cannot begin to take shape till it has this for its support. It seems obvious; yet there is nothing more familiar to a novel-reader of to-day than the difficulty of discovering what the novel in his hand is about. What was the novelist's intention, in a phrase? If it cannot be put into a phrase it is no subject for a novel; and the size or the complexity of a subject is in no way limited by that assertion. It may be the simplest anecdote or the most elaborate concatenation of events, it may be a solitary figure or the widest network of relationships; it is anyhow expressible in ten words that reveal its unity. The form of the book depends on it, and until it is known there is nothing to be said of the form.

IV

BUT now suppose that Tolstoy had not been
drawn aside from his first story in the midst of it,
suppose he had left the epic of his country and
"the historians" to be dealt with in another book,
suppose that the interpolated scenes of War and
Peace, as we possess it, were to disappear and to
leave the subject entirely to the young heroes
and heroines—what shall we find to be the form
of the book which is thus disencumbered? I
would try to think away from the novel all that
is not owned and dominated by these three
brilliant households, Besukhov, Bolkonsky, Rostov; there remains a long succession of scenes, in
a single and straightforward train of action. It is
still a novel of ample size; it spreads from the
moment when Peter, amiably uncouth, first
appears in a drawing-room of the social world, to
the evening, fifteen years later, when he is watched
with speechless veneration by the small boy
Nicolenka, herald of the future. The climax of
his life, the climax of half a dozen lives, is surmounted between these two points, and now
their story stands by itself. It gains, I could feel,
by this process of liberation, summary as it is.

At any rate, it is one theme and one book, and

the question of its form may be further pressed. The essential notion out of which this book sprang, I suggested, was that of the march of life, the shift of the generations in their order—a portentous subject to master, but Tolstoy's hand is broad and he is not afraid of great spaces. Such a subject could not be treated at all without a generous amount of room for its needs. It requires, to begin with, a big and various population; a few selected figures may hold the main thread of the story and represent its course, but it is necessary for their typical truth that their place in the world should be clearly seen. They are choice examples, standing away from the mass, but their meaning would be lost if they were taken to be utterly exceptional, if they appeared to be chosen *because* they are exceptional. Their attachment to the general drama of life must accordingly be felt and understood; the effect of a wide world must be given, opening away to far distances round the action of the centre. The whole point of the action is in its representative character, its universality; this it must plainly wear.

It begins to do so at once, from the very first. With less hesitation, apparently, than another man might feel in setting the scene of a street or parish, Tolstoy proceeds to make his world. Daylight seems to well out of his page and to surround his characters as fast as he sketches them; the darkness lifts from their lives, their conditions, their outlying affairs, and leaves them

44

under an open sky. In the whole of fiction no scene is so continually washed by the common air, free to us all, as the scene of Tolstoy. His people move in an atmosphere that knows no limit; beyond the few that are to the fore there stretches a receding crowd, with many faces in full light, and many more that are scarcely discerned as faces, but that swell the impression of swarming life. There is no perceptible horizon, no hard line between the life in the book and the life beyond it. The communication between the men and women of the story and the rest of the world is unchecked. It is impossible to say of Peter and Andrew and Nicholas that they inhabit a " world of their own," as the people in a story-book so often appear to do; they inhabit *our* world, like anybody else. I do not mean, of course, that a marked horizon, drawn round the action of a book and excluding everything that does not belong to it, is not perfectly appropriate, often enough; their own world may be all that the people need, may be the world that best reveals what they are to be and to do; it all depends on the nature of the fable. But to Tolstoy's fable space is essential, with the sense of the continuity of life, within and without the circle of the book. He never seems even to know that there can be any difficulty in providing it; while he writes, it is there.

He is helped, one might imagine, by the simple immensity of his Russian landscape, filled with the suggestion of distances and unending levels.

The Russian novelist who counts on this effect has it ready to his hand. If he is to render an impression of space that widens and widens, a hint is enough; the mere association of his picture with the thought of those illimitable plains might alone enlarge it to the utmost of his need. The imagination of distance is everywhere, not only in a free prospect, where sight is lost, but on any river-bank, where the course of the stream lies across a continent, or on the edge of a wood, whence the forest stretches round the curve of the globe. To isolate a patch of that huge field and to cut it off from the encompassing air might indeed seem to be the greater difficulty; how can the eye be held to a point when the very name of Russia is extent without measure? At our end of Europe, where space is more precious, life is divided and specialized and differentiated, but over there such economies are unnecessary; there is no need to define one's own world and to live within it when there is a single world large enough for all. The horizon of a Russian story would naturally be vague and vast, it might seem.

It might seem so, at least, if the fiction of Dostoevsky were not there with an example exactly opposed to the manner of Tolstoy. The serene and impartial day that arches from verge to verge in War and Peace, the blackness that hems in the ominous circle of the Brothers Karamazov—it is a perfect contrast. Dostoevsky needed no lucid prospect round his strange crew; all he sought was a blaze of light on the extraordinary theatre of their consciousness. He intensified it by shutting off the least glimmer of natural day. The illumination that falls upon his page is like the glare of a furnace-mouth; it searches the depths of the inner struggles and turmoils in which his drama is enacted, relieving it with sharp and fantastic shadows. That is all it requires, and therefore the curtain of darkness is drawn thickly over the rest of the world. Who can tell, in Dostoevsky's grim town-scenery, what there is at the end of the street, what lies round the next corner? Night stops the view—or rather no ordinary, earthly night, but a sudden opacity, a fog that cannot be pierced or breathed. With Tolstoy nobody doubts that an ample vision opens in every direction. It may be left untold, but his men and women have only to lift their eyes to see it.

How is it contrived? The mere multiplication of names and households in the book does not account for it; the effect I speak of spreads far beyond them. It is not that he has imagined so large an army of characters, it is that he manages to give them such freedom, such an obvious latitude of movement in the open world. Description has nothing to do with it; there is very little description in War and Peace, save in the battle-scenes that I am not now considering. And it is not enough to say that if Tolstoy's people have evident lives of their own, beyond the limits of the book, it is because he understands and knows them so well, because they are so " real " to him, because they and all their circumstances are so sharply present to his imagination. Who has ever known so much about his own creations as Balzac?—and who has ever felt that Balzac's people had the freedom of a bigger world than that very solid and definite habitation he made for them? There must be another explanation, and I think one may discern where it lies, though it would take me too far to follow it.

It lies perhaps in the fact that with Tolstoy's high poetic genius there went a singularly normal and everyday gift of experience. Genius of his sort generally means, I dare say, that the possessor of it is struck by special and wonderful aspects of the world; his vision falls on it from a peculiar angle, cutting into unsuspected sides of common facts—as a painter sees a quality in a face that other people never saw. So it is with Balzac, and so it is, in their different ways, with such writers as Stendhal and Maupassant, or again as Dickens and Meredith; they all create a " world of their own." Tolstoy seems to look squarely at the same world as other people, and only to make so much more of it than other people by the direct force of his genius, not because he holds a different position in regard to it. His experience comes from the same quarter as ours; it is because he absorbs so much more of it, and because it all passes into his great plastic imagination, that it seems so new. His people, therefore, are essentially familiar and intelligible; we easily

extend their lives in any direction, instead of
finding ourselves checked by the difficulty of
knowing more about them than the author tells
us in so many words. Of this kind of genius I
take Tolstoy to be the supreme instance among
novelists; Fielding and Scott and Thackeray are
of the family. But I do not linger over a matter
that for my narrow argument is a side-issue.

The continuity of space and of daylight, then,
so necessary to the motive of the book, is rendered
in War and Peace with absolute mastery. There
is more, or there is not so much, to be said of the
way in which the long flight of time through the
expanse of the book is imagined and pictured.
The passage of time, the effect of time, belongs
to the heart of the subject; if we could think of
War and Peace as a book still to be written, this,
no doubt, would seem to be the greatest of its
demands. The subject is not given at all unless
the movement of the wheel of time is made
perceptible. I suppose there is nothing that is
more difficult to ensure in a novel. Merely to
lengthen the series of stages and developments in
the action will not ensure it; there is no help in
the simple ranging of fact beside fact, to suggest
the lapse of a certain stretch of time; a novelist
might as well fall back on the row of stars and
the unsupported announcement that " years have
fled." It is a matter of the build of the whole
book. The form of time is to be represented, and
that is something more than to represent its
contents in their order. If time is of the essence

THE CRAFT OF FICTION

of the book, the lines and masses of the book must show it.

Time is all-important in War and Peace, but that does not necessarily mean that it will cover a great many years; they are in fact no more than the years between youth and middle age. But though the wheel may not travel very far in the action as we see it, there must be no doubt of the great size of the wheel; it must seem to turn in a large circumference, though only a part of its journey is to be watched. The revolution of life marked by the rising and sinking of a certain generation—such is the story; and the years that Tolstoy treats, fifteen or so, may be quite enough to show the sweep of the curve. At five-and-twenty a man is still beginning; at forty —I do not say that at forty he is already ending, though Tolstoy in his ruthless way is prepared to suggest it; but by that time there are clear and intelligent eyes, like the boy Nicolenka's, fixed enquiringly upon a man—the eyes of the new-comers, who are suddenly everywhere and all about him, making ready to begin in their turn. As soon as that happens the curve of time is apparent, the story is told. But it must be *made* apparent in the book; the shape of the story must give the reason for telling it, the purpose of the author in chronicling his facts.

Can we feel that Tolstoy has so represented the image of time, the part that time plays in his book? The problem was twofold; there was first of all the steady progression, the accumulation of the years, to be portrayed, and then the rise and fall of their curve. It is the double effect of time —its uninterrupted lapse, and the cycle of which the chosen stretch is a segment. I cannot think there is much doubt about the answer to my question. Tolstoy has achieved one aspect of his handful of years with rare and exquisite art, he has troubled himself very little about the other. Time that evenly and silently slips away, while the men and women talk and act and forget it— time that is read in their faces, in their gestures, in the changing texture of their thought, while they only themselves awake to the discovery that it is passing when the best of it has gone—time in this aspect is present in War and Peace more manifestly, perhaps, than in any other novel that could be named, unless it were another novel of Tolstoy's. In so far as it is a matter of the *length* of his fifteen years, they are there in the story with their whole effect.

He is the master of the changes of age in a human being. Under his hand young men and women grow older, cease to be young, grow old, with the noiseless regularity of life; their muta- bility never hides their sameness, their consistency shows and endures through their disintegration. They grow as we all do, they change in the only possible direction, that which results from the clash between themselves and their conditions. If I looked for the most beautiful illustration in all fiction of a woman at the mercy of time, exposed to the action of the years, now facing it with what she is, presently betraying and recording it with what she becomes, I should surely find it in the story of Anna Karenina. Various and exquisite as she is, her whole nature is sensitive to the imprint of time, and the way in which time invades her, steals throughout her, finally lays her low, Tolstoy tracks and renders from end to end. And in War and Peace his hand is not less delicate and firm. The progress of time is never broken; inexorably it does what it must, carrying an enthusiastic young student forward into a slatternly philosopher of middle life, linking an over-blown matron with the memory of a girl dancing into a crowded room. The years move on and on, there is no missing the sense of their flow.

But the meaning, the import, what I should like to call the moral of it all—what of that? Tolstoy has shown us a certain length of time's journey, but to what end has he shown it? The question has to be answered, and it is not answered, it is only postponed, if we say that the picture itself is all the moral, all the meaning that we are entitled to ask for. It is of the picture that we speak; its moral is in its design, and without design the scattered scenes will make no picture. Our answer would be clear enough, as I have tried to suggest, if we could see in the form of the novel an image of the circling sweep of time. But to a broad and single effect, such as that, the chapters of the book refuse to adapt themselves; they will not draw together and announce a reason for their collocation. The story is started with every promise, and it ceases at the end with an air of considerable finality. But between these points its course is full of doubt.

It is admirably started. Nothing could be more right and true than the bubbling merriment and the good faith and the impatient aspiration with which the young life of the earlier chapters of the book comes surging upon the scene of its elders. A current of newness and freshness is set flowing in the atmosphere of the generation that is still in possession. The talk of a political drawing-room is stale and shrill, an old man in his seclusion is a useless encumbrance, an easy-going and conventional couple are living without plan or purpose—all the futility of these people is obvious to an onlooker from the moment when their sons and daughters break in upon them. It was time for the new generation to appear—and behold it appearing in lively strength. Tolstoy, with his power of making an eloquent event out of nothing at all, needs no dramatic apparatus to set off the effect of the irruption. Two people, an elderly man of the world and a scheming hostess, are talking together, the room fills, a young man enters; or in another sociable assembly there is a shriek and a rush, and the children of the house charge into the circle; that is quite enough for Tolstoy, his drama of youth and age opens immediately with the right impression. The story is in movement without delay; there are a few glimpses of this kind, and then the scene is ready, the action may go forward; everything is attuned for the effect it is to make.

And at the other end of the book, after many hundreds of pages, the story is brought to a full close in an episode which gathers up all the threads and winds them together. The youths and maidens are now the parents of another riotous brood. Not one of them has ended where he or she expected to end, but their lives have taken a certain shape, and it is unmistakable that this shape is final. Nothing more will happen to them which an onlooker cannot easily foretell. They have settled down upon their lines, and very comfortable and very estimable lines on the whole, and there may be many years of prosperity before them; but they no longer possess the future that was sparkling with possibility a few years ago. Peter is as full of schemes as ever, but who now supposes that he will *do* anything? Natasha is absorbed in her children like a motherly hen; Nicholas, the young cavalier, is a country gentleman; they are all what they were bound to be, though nobody foresaw it. But shyly lurking in a corner, late in the evening, with eyes fixed upon the elders of the party who are talking and arguing—here once more is that same uncertain, romantic, incalculable future; the last word is with the new generation, the budding morrow, old enough now to be musing and speculating over its own visions. " Yes, I will do such things—!" says Nicolenka; and that is the natural end of the story.

But meanwhile the story has rambled and wandered uncontrolled—or controlled only by Tolstoy's perfect consistency in the treatment of his characters. They, as I have said, are never less than absolutely true to themselves; wherever we meet them, in peace or war, they are always the people we know, the same as ever, and yet changing and changing (like all the people we know) under the touch of time. It is not they, it is their story that falters. The climax, I suppose, must be taken to fall in the great scenes of the burning of Moscow, with which all their lives are so closely knit. Peter involves himself in a tangle of misfortunes (as he would, of course) by his slipshod enthusiasm; Natasha's courage and good sense are surprisingly aroused—one had hardly seen that she possessed such qualities, but Tolstoy is right; and presently it is Andrew, the one clear-headed and far-sighted member of the circle, who is lost to it in the upheaval, wounded and brought home to die. It is a beautiful and human story of its kind; but note that it has entirely dropped the representative character which it wore at the beginning and is to pick up again at the end. Tolstoy has forgotten about this; partly he has been too much engrossed in his historical picture, and partly he has fallen into a new manner of handling the loves and fortunes of his young people. It is now a tale of a group of men and women, with their cross-play of affinities, a tale of which the centre of interest lies in the way in which their mutual relations will work out. It is the kind of story we expect to find in any novel, a drama of young affections —extraordinarily true and poetic, as Tolstoy traces it, but a limited affair compared with the theme of his first chapters.

Of that theme there is no continuous development. The details of the charming career of Natasha, for example, have no bearing on it at all. Natasha is the delightful girl of her time and of all time, as Nicholas is the delightful boy, and she runs through the sequence of moods and love-affairs that she properly should; she is one whose fancy is quick and who easily follows it. But in the large drama of which she is a part it is not the actual course of her love-affairs that has any importance, it is the fact that she has them, that she is what she is, that every one loves her and that she is ready to love nearly every one. To do as Tolstoy does, to bring into the middle of the interest the question whether she will marry this man or that—especially when it is made as exquisitely interesting as he makes it—this is to throw away the value that she had and to give her another of a different sort entirely. At the turning-point of the book, and long before the turning-point is reached, she is simply the heroine of a particular story; what she *had* been—Tolstoy made it quite clear—was the heroine of a much more general story, when she came dancing in on the crest of the new wave.

It is a change of attitude and of method on

Tolstoy's part. He sees the facts of his story from a different point of view and represents them in a fresh light. It does not mean that he modifies their course, that he forces them in a wrong direction and makes Natasha act in a manner conflicting with his first idea. She acts and behaves consistently with her nature, exactly as the story demands that she should; not one of her impulsive proceedings need be sacrificed. But it was for Tolstoy, representing them, to behave consistently too, and to use the facts in accordance with his purpose. He had a reason for taking them in hand, a design which he meant them to express; and his vacillation prevents them from expressing it. How would he have treated the story, supposing that he had kept hold of his original reason throughout? Are we prepared to improve upon his method, to re-write his book as we think it ought to have been written? Well, at any rate, it is possible to imagine the different effect it would show if a little of that large, humane irony, so evident in the tone of the story at the start, had persisted through all its phases. It would not have dimmed Natasha's charm, it would have heightened it. While she is simply the heroine of a romance she is enchanting, no doubt; but when she takes her place in a drama so much greater than herself, her beauty is infinitely enhanced. She becomes representative, with all her gifts and attractions; she is there, not because she is a beautiful creature, but because she is the spirit of youth.

Her charm is then universal; it belongs to the spirit of youth and lasts for ever.

With all this I think it begins to be clear why the broad lines of Tolstoy's book have always seemed uncertain and confused. Neither his subject nor his method were fixed for him as he wrote; he ranged around his mountain of material, attacking it now here and now there, never deciding in his mind to what end he had amassed it. None of his various schemes is thus completed, none of them gets the full advantage of the profusion of life which he commands. At any moment great masses of that life are being wasted, turned to no account; and the result is not merely negative, for at any moment the wasted life, the stuff that is not being used, is dividing and weakening the effect of the picture created out of the rest. That so much remains, in spite of everything, gives the measure of Tolstoy's genius; *that* becomes the more extra-ordinary as the chaotic plan of his book is explored. He could work with such lordly neglect of his subject and yet he could produce such a book—it is surely as much as to say that Tolstoy's is the supreme genius among novelists.

V

AND next of the different methods by which the form of a novel is created—these must be watched in a very different kind of book from Tolstoy's. For a sight of the large and general masses in which a novel takes shape, War and Peace seemed to promise more than another; but something a great deal more finely controlled is to be looked for, when it is a question of following the novelist's hand while it is actually at work. Not indeed that anybody's hand is more delicate than Tolstoy's at certain moments and for certain effects, and a critic is bound to come back to him again in connection with these. But we have seen how, in dealing with his book, one is continually distracted by the question of its subject; the uncertainty of Tolstoy's intention is always getting between the reader and the detail of his method. What I now want, therefore, will be a book in which the subject is absolutely fixed and determined, so that it may be possible to consider the manner of its treatment with undivided attention. It is not so easy to find as might be supposed; or rather it might be difficult to find, but for the fact that immediately in a critic's path, always ready to hand and unavoidable, there lies one book of exactly the sort I seek,

59

Flaubert's Madame Bovary. Whatever this book may be or may not be, after much re-reading, it remains perpetually the novel of all novels which the criticism of fiction cannot overlook; as soon as ever we speak of the principles of the art, we must be prepared to engage with Flaubert.

This is an accepted necessity among critics, and no doubt there is every reason why it should be so. The art of Flaubert gives at any rate a perfectly definite standard; there is no mistaking or mis-reading it. He is not of those who present many aspects, offering the support of one or other to different critical doctrines; Flaubert has only one word to say, and it is impossible to find more than a single meaning in it. He establishes accordingly a point in the sphere of criticism, a point which is convenient to us all; we can refer to it at any time, in the full assurance that its position is the same in everybody's view; he provides the critic with a motionless pole. And for my particular purpose, just now, there is no such book as his Bovary; for it is a novel in which the subject stands firm and clear, without the least shade of ambiguity to break the line which bounds it. The story of its treatment may be traced without missing a single link.

It is copiously commented upon, as we know, in the published letters of its author, through the long years in which phrase was being added to phrase; and it is curious indeed to listen to him day by day, and to listen in vain for any hint of trouble or embarrassment in the matter of his subject. He was capable of hating and reviling his unfortunate story, and of talking about it with a kind of exasperated spite, as though it had somehow got possession of him unfairly and he owed it a grudge for having crossed his mind. That is strange enough, but that is quite a different affair; his personal resentment of the intrusion of such a book upon him had nothing to do with the difficulty he found in writing it. His classic agonies were caused by no unruliness in the story he had to tell; his imagined book was rooted in his thought, and never left its place by a hair's breadth. Year after year he worked upon his subject without finding anything in it, apparently, to disturb or distract him in his continuous effort to treat it, to write it out to his satisfaction. This was the only difficulty; there was no question of struggling with a subject that he had not entirely mastered, one that broke out with unforeseen demands; Bovary never needed to be held down with one hand while it was written with the other. Many a novelist, making a further and fuller acquaintance with his subject as he proceeds, discovering more in it to reckon with than he had expected, has to meet the double strain, it would seem. But Flaubert kept his book in a marvellous state of quiescence during the writing of it; through all the torment which it cost him there was no hour when it presented a new or uncertain look to him. He might hate his subject, but it never disappointed or disconcerted him.

In Bovary, accordingly, the methods of the art are thrown into clear relief. The story stands obediently before the author, with all its developments and illustrations, the characters defined, the small incidents disposed in order. His sole thought is how to present the story, how to tell it in a way that will give the effect he desires, how to show the little collection of facts so that they may announce the meaning he sees in them. I speak of his " telling " the story, but of course he has no idea of doing that and no more; the art of fiction does not begin until the novelist thinks of his story as a matter to be *shown*, to be so exhibited that it will tell itself. To hand over to the reader the facts of the story merely as so much information—this is no more than to state the " argument " of the book, the groundwork upon which the novelist proceeds to create. The book is not a row of facts, it is a single image; the facts have no validity in themselves, they are nothing until they have been used. It is not the simple art of narrative, but the comprehensive art of fiction that I am considering; and in fiction there can be no appeal to any authority outside the book itself. Narrative— like the tales of Defoe, for example—must look elsewhere for support; Defoe produced it by the assertion of the historic truthfulness of his stories. But in a novel, strictly so called, attestation of this kind is, of course, quite irrelevant; the thing has to *look* true, and that is all. It is not made to look true by simple statement.

And yet the novelist must state, must tell, must narrate—what else can he do? His book is a series of assertions, nothing more. It is so, obviously, and the difference between the art of Defoe and the art of Flaubert is only in their different method of placing their statements. Defoe takes a directer way, Flaubert a more roundabout; but the deviations open to Flaubert are innumerable, and by his method, by his various methods, we mean his manner of choosing his path. Having chosen he follows it, certainly, by means of a plain narrative; he relates a succession of facts, whether he is describing the appearance of Emma, or one of her moods, or something that she did. But this common necessity of statement, at the bottom of it all, is assumed at the beginning; and in criticizing fiction we may proceed as though a novelist could really deal immediately with appearances. We may talk of the picture or the drama that he creates, we may plainly say that he avoids mere statement altogether, because at the level of fiction the whole interest is in another region; we are simply concerned with the method by which he selects the information he offers. A writer like Flaubert—or like any novelist whose work supports criticism at all—is so far from telling a story as it might be told in an official report, that we cease to regard him as reporting in any sense. He is making an effect and an impression, by some more or less skilful method. Contemplating his finished work we can distinguish the method, perhaps define it, notice how it changes from time to time, and account for the novelist's choice of it.

There is plenty of diversity of method in Madame Bovary, though the story is so simple. What does it amount to, that story? Charles Bovary, a simple and slow-witted young country doctor, makes a prudent marriage, and has the fortune to lose his tiresome and elderly wife after no long time. Then he falls in love with the daughter of a neighbouring farmer, a pretty and fanciful young woman, who marries him. She is deeply bored by existence in a small market town, finds a lover, wearies him and finds another, gets wildly into debt, poisons herself and dies. After her death Bovary discovers the proof of her infidelity, but his slow brain is too much bewildered by sorrow and worry, by life generally, to feel another pang very distinctly. He soon dies himself. That is all the story, given as an " argument," and so summarized it tells us nothing of Flaubert's subject. There might be many subjects in such an anecdote, many different points of view from which the commonplace facts might make a book. The way in which they are presented will entirely depend on the particular subject that Flaubert sees in them; until this is apparent the method cannot be criticized.

But the method can be watched; and immediately it is to be noted that Flaubert handles his material quite differently from point to point.

Sometimes he seems to be describing what he has seen himself, places and people he has known, conversations he may have overheard; I do not mean that he is literally retailing an experience of his own, but that he writes as though he were. His description, in that case, touches only such matters as you or I might have perceived for ourselves, if we had happened to be on the spot at the moment. His object is to place the scene before us, so that we may take it in like a picture gradually unrolled or a drama enacted. But then again the method presently changes. There comes a juncture at which, for some reason, it is necessary for us to know more than we could have made out by simply looking and listening. Flaubert, the author of the story, must intervene with his superior knowledge. Perhaps it is something in the past of the people who have been moving and talking on the scene; you cannot rightly understand this incident or this talk, the author implies, unless you know—what I now proceed to tell you. And so, for a new light on the drama, the author recalls certain circumstances that we should otherwise have missed. Or it may be that he—who naturally knows everything, even the inmost, unexpressed thought of the characters—wishes us to share the mind of Bovary or of Emma, not to wait only on their words or actions; and so he goes below the surface, enters their consciousness, and describes the train of sentiment that passes there.

These are the familiar resources of a story-

THE CRAFT OF FICTION

teller, which everybody uses as a matter of
course. It is so natural to take advantage of
them that unless we purposely keep an eye upon
the writer's devices, marking them off as he turns
from one to another, we hardly notice the change.
He is telling a story in the ordinary way, the
obvious and unconstrained. But in fact these
variations represent differences of method that
are fundamental. If the story is to be *shown* to us,
the question of our relation to the story, how we
are placed with regard to it, arises with the first
word. Are we placed before a particular scene,
an occasion, at a certain selected hour in the lives
of these people whose fortunes are to be followed?
Or are we surveying their lives from a height,
participating in the privilege of the novelist—
sweeping their history with a wide range of
vision and absorbing a general effect? Here at
once is a necessary alternative. Flaubert, as a
matter of fact, gives us first a scene—the scene
of Bovary's arrival at school, as a small boy;
the incident of the particular morning is rendered;
and then he leaves that incident, summarizes the
background of the boy's life, describes his
parents, the conditions of his home, his later
career as a student. It is the way in which nine
novels out of ten begin—an opening scene, a
retrospect, and a summary. And the spectator,
the reader, is so well used to it that he is conscious
of no violent change in the point of view; though
what has happened is that from one moment to
another he has been caught up from a position

straight in front of the action to a higher and a more commanding level, from which a stretch of time is to be seen outspread. This, then, is one distinction of method; and it is a tell-tale fact that even in this elementary matter our nomenclature is uncertain and ambiguous. How do we habitually discriminate between these absolutely diverse manners of presenting the facts of a story? I scarcely know—it is as though we had no received expressions to mark the difference between blue and red. But let us assume, at any rate, that a " scenic " and a " panoramic " presentation of a story expresses an intelligible antithesis, strictly and technically.

There is our relation, again—ours, the reader's —with regard to the author. Flaubert is generally considered to be a very " impersonal " writer, one who keeps in the background and desires us to remain unaware of his presence; he places the story before us and suppresses any comment of his own. But this point has been over-laboured, I should say; it only means that Flaubert does not announce his opinion in so many words, and thence it has been argued that the opinions of a really artistic writer ought not to appear in his story at all. But of course with every touch that he lays on his subject he must show what he thinks of it; his subject, indeed, the book which he finds in his selected fragment of life, is purely the representation of his view, his judgement, his opinion of it. The famous " impersonality " of Flaubert and his kind lies only in the greater tact with which they express their feelings—dramatizing them, embodying them in living form, instead of stating them directly. It is not to this matter, Flaubert's opinion of Emma Bovary and her history—which indeed is unmistakable—that I refer in speaking of our relation to the writer of the book.

It is a matter of method. Sometimes the author is talking with his own voice, sometimes he is talking *through* one of the people in the book—in this book for the most part Emma herself. Thus he describes a landscape, the trim country-side in which Emma's lot is cast, or the appearance and manners of her neighbours, or her own behaviour; and in so doing he is using his own language and his own standards of appreciation; he is facing the reader in person, however careful he may be to say nothing to deflect our attention from the thing described. He is making a reproduction of something that is in his own mind. And then later on he is using the eyes and the mind and the standards of another; the landscape has now the colour that it wears in Emma's view, the incident is caught in the aspect which it happens to turn towards her imagination. Flaubert himself has retreated, and it is Emma with whom we immediately deal. Take, for example, the two figures of her lovers, Rodolphe and Léon, the florid country-gentleman and the aspiring student; if Flaubert were to describe these men as *he* sees them, apart from their significance to Emma, they would not occupy him for long; to his mind, and to any critical mind, they are both of them very small affairs. Their whole effect in the book is the effect they produce upon the sensibility of a foolish and limited little woman. Or again, take the incident of Emma's single incursion into polite society, the ball at the great house which starts so many of her romantic dreams; it is all presented in her terms, it appears as it appeared to her. And occasionally the point of view is shifted away from her to somebody else, and we get a brief glimpse of what *she* is in the eyes of her husband, her mother-in-law, her lover.

Furthermore, whether the voice is that of the author or of his creature, there is a pictorial manner of treating the matter in hand and there is also a dramatic. It may be that the impression —as in the case of the marquis's ball—is chiefly given as a picture, the reflection of events in the mirror of somebody's receptive consciousness. The reader is not really looking *at* the occasion in the least, or only now and then; mainly he is watching the surge of Emma's emotion, on which the episode acts with sharp intensity. The thing is " scenic," in the sense in which I used the word just now; we are concerned, that is to say, with a single and particular hour, we are taking no extended, general view of Emma's experience. But though it is thus a *scene*, it is not dramatically rendered; if you took the dialogue, what there is of it, together with the actual things described, the people and the dresses and the dances and the banquets—took these and placed them on the stage, for a theatrical performance, the peculiar effect of the occasion in the book would totally vanish. Nothing could be more definite, more objective, than the scene is in the book; but there it is all bathed in the climate of Emma's mood, and it is to the nature of this climate that our interest is called for the moment. The lords and ladies are remote, Emma's envying and wondering excitement fills the whole of the foreground. The scene is pictorially treated.

But then look on to the incident of the *comices agricoles*, the cattle-show at Yonville, with the crowd in the market-place, the prize-giving and the speech-making. This scene, like the other, is rendered on the whole (but Flaubert's method is always a little mixed, for reasons to be noted presently) from Emma's point of view; she sits beside Rodolphe, while he makes his advances to her under cover of the councillor's eloquence, and she looks out upon the assembly—and as she sees it, so the throng and the glare are imparted to the reader. But remark that on this occasion the facts of the scene are well to the fore; Emma's mood counts for very little, and we get a direct view of the things on which her eyes casually rest. We hear the councillor's rhetorical periods, Rodolphe's tender speeches, Emma's replies, with the rumour of the crowd breaking through from time to time. It is a scene which might be put upon the stage, quite conceivably, without any loss of the main impression it is made to convey in the book—an impression of ironic contrast, of the bustle and jostle round the oration of the pompous dignitary, of the commonplace little romance that is being broached unobserved. To receive the force of the contrast the reader has only to see and hear, to be present while the hour passes; and the author places him there accordingly, in front of the visible and audible facts of the case, and leaves it to these to tell the story. It is a scene treated dramatically.

This is a difference of method that constantly catches a critic's eye in reading a novel. Is the author writing, at a given moment, with his attention upon the incidents of his tale, or is he regarding primarily the form and colour they assume in somebody's thought? He will do both, it is probable, in the course of his book, on the same page, perhaps, or even in the same sentence; nothing compels him to forego the advantage of either method, if his story can profit in turn from both. Now and then, indeed, we shall find a writer deliberately confining himself to one method only, treating his whole book with a rigid consistency, and this for the sake of some particular aspect of his theme which an unmixed manner is best fitted to reveal. But generally a novelist retains his liberty to draw upon any of his resources as he chooses, now this one and now that, using drama where drama gives him all he needs, using pictorial description where the turn of the story demands it. The only law that binds him throughout, whatever course he is pursuing, is the need to be consistent on *some* plan, to follow the principle he has adopted; and of course it is one of the first of his precepts, as with every artist in any kind, to allow himself no more latitude than he requires. A critic, then, looks for the principle on which a novelist's methods are mingled and varied—looks for it, as usual, in the novelist's subject, and marks its application as the subject is developed.

And so with the devices that I distinguish as scenic and panoramic—one watches continually to see how this alternation is managed, how the story is now overlooked from a height and now brought immediately to the level of the reader. Here again the need of the story may sometimes seem to pull decisively in one direction or the other; and we get a book that is mainly a broad and general survey, or mainly a concatenation of particular scenes. But on the whole we expect to find that the scene presently yields to some kind of chronicle or summary, and that this in turn prepares the way and leads into the occasion that fulfils it. The placing of this occasion, at the point where everything is ready for it, where it will thoroughly illuminate a new face of the subject and advance the action by a definite stage, is among the chief cares of the author, I take it, in planning his book. A scene that is not really wanted, and that *does* nothing in particular —a scene that for lack of preparation fails to make its effect—is a weakness in a story that one would suppose a novelist to be always guarding against. Anyhow there is no doubt that the scene holds the place of honour, that it is the readiest means of starting an interest and raising a question—we drop into a scene on the first page and begin to speculate about the people concerned in it: and that it recurs for a climax of any sort, the resolution of the question—and so the scene completes what it began. In Madame Bovary the scenes are distributed and rendered with very rare skill; not one but seems to have more and more to give with every fresh reading of it. The ball, the *comices*, the evening at the theatre, Emma's fateful interview with Léon in the Cathedral of Rouen, the remarkable session of the priest and the apothecary at her deathbed —these form the articulation of the book, the scheme of its structure. To the next in order each stage of the story is steadily directed. By the time the scene is reached, nothing is wanting to its opportunity; the action is ripe, the place is resonant; and then the incident takes up the story, conclusively establishes one aspect of it and opens the view towards the next. And the more rapid summary that succeeds, with its pauses for a momentary sight of Emma's daily life and its setting, carries the book on once more to the climax that already begins to appear in the distance.

But the most obvious point of method is no doubt the difficult question of the centre of vision. With which of the characters, if with any of them, is the writer to identify himself, which

73

is he to " go behind " ? Which of these vessels of thought and feeling is he to reveal from within ? I suppose his unwritten story to rise before him, its main lines settled, as something at first entirely objective, the whole thing seen from without—the linked chain of incident, the men and women in their places. And it may be that the story can be kept in this condition while it is written, and that the completed book will be nothing but an account of things seen from the point of view of the author, standing outside the action, without any divulging of anybody's thought. But this is rare; such restraint is burdensome, unless in a very compact and straightforward tale. Somewhere the author must break into the privacy of his characters and open their minds to us. And again it is doubtless his purpose to shift the point of view no more often than he need; and if the subject can be completely rendered by showing it as it appears to a single one of the figures in the book, then there is no reason to range further. Haphazard and unnecessary plunges into the inner life of the characters only confuse the effect, changing the focus without compensating gain. But which *is* the centre, which is the mind that really commands the subject? The answer is not always evident at once, nor does it seem to be always correctly divined in the novels that we read. But of course in plenty of stories there can be little doubt; there is somebody in the middle of the action who is clearly the person to interpret it for us, and the action will accordingly be faced from his or her position. In Flaubert's Bovary there could be no question but that we must mainly use the eyes of Emma herself; the middle of the subject is in her experience, not anywhere in the concrete facts around her. And yet Flaubert finds it necessary, as I said, to look *at* her occasionally, taking advantage of some other centre for the time being; and why he does so a nearer inspection of his subject will soon show.

Here we have, then, the elements of the novelist's method—essentially few and simple, but infinite in their possibilities of fusion and combination. They are arranged in a new design to suit every new theme that a writer takes in hand; we see them alternated, united, imposed one on another, this point of view blended with that, dramatic action treated pictorially, pictorial description rendered dramatically—and these words I use throughout, it will be understood, in the special sense that I have indicated. In well-fashioned work it is always interesting to discover how method tends to be laid upon method, so that we get, as it were, layers and stratifications in the treatment of a story. Some of these I shall try to distinguish, and the search is useful, I think, for an understanding of the novelist himself. For though it is true that a man's method depends upon the particular story he is engaged in telling, yet the story that occurs to him, the subject he happens upon, will be that which asks for the kind of treatment congenial to his hand; and so his method will be a part of himself, and will tell us about the quality of his imagination. But this by the way—my concern is only with the manner in which the thing is done; and having glanced at some of the features of that manner in Flaubert's Bovary, I may now seek the reason of them in a more attentive handling of the book.

VI

IF Flaubert allows himself the liberty of telling his story in various ways—with a method, that is to say, which is often modified as he proceeds— it is likely that he has good cause to do so. Weighing every word and calculating every effect so patiently, he could not have been casual and careless over his method; he would not take one way rather than another because it saved him trouble, or because he failed to notice that there were other ways, or because they all seemed to him much the same. And yet at first sight it does seem that his manner of arriving at his subject—if his subject is Emma Bovary—is considerably casual. He begins with Charles, of all people—Charles, her husband, the stupid soul who falls heavily in love with her prettiness and never has the glimmer of an understanding of what she is; and he begins with the early history of Charles, and his upbringing, and the irrelevant first marriage that his mother forces upon him, and his widowhood; and then it happens that Charles has a professional visit to pay to a certain farm, the farmer's daughter happens to be Emma, and so we finally stumble upon the subject of the book. Is that the neatest possible

THE CRAFT OF FICTION

mode of striking it? But Flaubert seems to be
very sure of himself, and it is not uninteresting
to ask exactly what he means.

As for his subject, it is of course Emma
Bovary in the first place; the book is the portrait
of a foolish woman, romantically inclined, in
small and prosaic conditions. She is in the centre
of it all, certainly; there is no doubt of her position in the book. But *why* is she there? The true
subject of the novel is not given, as we saw, by
a mere summary of the course which is taken by
the story. She may be there for her own sake,
simply, or for the sake of the predicament in
which she stands; she may be presented as a
curious scrap of character, fit to be studied; or
Flaubert may have been struck by her as the
instrument, the victim, the occasion, of a particular train of events. Perhaps she is a creature
portrayed because he thinks her typical and
picturesque; perhaps she is a disturbing little
force let loose among the lives that surround her;
perhaps, on the other hand, she is a hapless
sufferer in the clash between her aspirations and
her fate. Given Emma and what she is by nature,
given her environment and the facts of her story,
there are dozens of different subjects, I dare say,
latent in the case. The woman, the men, all they
say and do, the whole scene behind them—none
of it gives any clue to the right manner of treating
them. The one irreducible idea out of which the
book, as Flaubert wrote it, unfolds—this it is
that must be sought.

Now if Emma was devised for her own sake, solely because a nature and a temper like hers seemed to Flaubert an amusing study—if his one aim was to make the portrait of a woman of that kind—then the rest of the matter falls into line, we shall know how to regard it. These conditions in which Emma finds herself will have been chosen by the author because they appeared to throw light on her, to call out her natural qualities, to give her the best opportunity of disclosing what she is. Her stupid husband and her fascinating lovers will enter the scene in order that she may become whatever she has it in her to be. Flaubert elects to place her in a certain provincial town, full of odd characters; he gives the town and its folk an extraordinary actuality; it is not a town *quelconque*, not a generalized town, but as individual and recognizable as he can make it. None the less—always supposing that Emma by herself is the whole of his subject—he must have lit on this particular town simply because it seemed to explain and expound her better than another. If he had thought that a woman of her sort, rather meanly ambitious, rather fatuously romantic, would have revealed her quality more intensely in a different world—in success, freedom, wealth—he would have placed her otherwise; Charles and Rodolphe and Homard and the rest of them would have vanished, the more illuminating set of circumstances (whatever they might be) would have appeared instead. Emma's world as it is at present, in the book that

79

Flaubert wrote, would have to be regarded, accordingly, as all a *consequence* of Emma, invented to do her a service, described in order that they may make the description of *her*. Her world, that is to say, would belong to the treatment of the story; none of it, not her husband, not the life of the market-town, would be a part of the author's postulate, the groundwork of his fable; it would be possible to imagine a different setting, better, it might be, than that which Flaubert has chosen. All this—*if* the subject of the book is nothing but the portrait of such a woman.

But of course it is not so; one glance at our remembrance of the book is enough to show it. Emma's world could not be other than it is, she could not be shifted into richer and larger conditions, without destroying the whole point and purpose of Flaubert's novel. She by herself is not the subject of his book. What he proposes to exhibit is the history of a woman like her in just such a world as hers, a foolish woman in narrow circumstances; so that the provincial scene, acting upon her, making her what she becomes, is as essential as she is herself. Not a portrait, therefore, not a study of character for its own sake, but something in the nature of a drama, where the two chief players are a woman on one side and her whole environment on the other— that is Madame Bovary. There is a conflict, a trial of strength, and a doubtful issue. Emma is not much of a force, no doubt; her impulses are wild, her emotions are thin and poor, she has no power of passion with which to fight the world. All she has is her romantic dream and her plain, primitive appetite; but these can be effective arms, after all, and she may yet succeed in getting her way and making her own terms. On the other hand the limitations of her life are very blank and uncompromising indeed; they close all round her, hampering her flights, restricting her opportunities. The drama is set, at any rate, whatever may come of it; Emma marries her husband, is established at Yonville and faced with the poverty of her situation. Something will result, the issue will announce itself. It is the mark of a dramatic case that it contains an opposition of some kind, a pair of wills that collide, an action that pulls in two directions; and so far Madame Bovary has the look of a drama. Flaubert might work on the book from that point of view and throw the emphasis on the issue. The middle of his subject would then be found in the struggle between Emma and all that constitutes her life, between her romantic dreams and her besetting facts. The question is what will happen.

But then again—that is not exactly the question in this book. Obviously the emphasis is not upon the commonplace little events of Emma's career. They might, no doubt, be the steps in a dramatic tale, but they are nothing of the kind as Flaubert handles them. He makes it perfectly clear that his view is not centred upon the actual outcome of Emma's predicament, whether it will issue this way or that; *what* she does or fails to do is of very small moment. Her passages with Rodolphe and with Léon are pictures that pass; they solve nothing, they lead to no climax. Rodolphe's final rejection of her, for example, is no scene of drama, deciding a question that has been held in suspense; it is one of Emma's various mischances, with its own marked effect upon *her*, but it does not stand out in the book as a turning-point in the action. She goes her way and acts out her history; but of whatever suspense, whatever dramatic value, there might be in it Flaubert makes nothing, he evidently considers it of no account. Who, in recalling the book, thinks of the chain of incident that runs through it, compared with the long and living impression of a few of the people in it and of the place in which they are set? None of the events really matter for their own sake; they might have happened differently, not one of them is indispensable as it is. Emma must certainly have made what she could of her opportunities of romance, but they need not necessarily have appeared in the shape of Léon or Rodolphe; she would have found others if these had not been at hand. The *events*, therefore, Emma's excursions to Rouen, her forest-rides, her one or two memorable adventures in the world, all these are only Flaubert's way of telling his subject, of making it count to the eye. They are not in themselves what he has to say, they simply illustrate it.

What it comes to, I take it, is that though

THE CRAFT OF FICTION

Madame Bovary, the novel, is a kind of drama—
since there is the interaction of this woman confronted by these facts—it is a drama chosen for
the sake of the picture in it, for the impression it
gives of the manner in which certain lives are
lived. It might have another force of its own; it
might be a strife of characters and wills, in which
the men and women would take the matter into
their own hands and make all the interest by
their action; it might be a drama, say, as Jane
Eyre is a drama, where another obscure little
woman has a part to play, but where the question
is how she plays it, what she achieves or misses
in particular. To Flaubert the situation out of
which he made his novel appeared in another
light. It was not as dramatic as it was pictorial;
there was not the stuff in Emma, more especially,
that could make her the main figure of a drama;
she is small and futile, she could not well uphold
an interest that would depend directly on her
behaviour. But for a picture, where the interest
depends only on what she *is*—that is quite
different. Her futility is then a real value; it can
be made amusing and vivid to the last degree,
so long as no other weight is thrown on it; she
can make a perfect impression of life, though
she cannot create much of a story. Let Emma
and her plight, therefore, appear as a picture;
let her be shown in the act of living her life,
entangled as it is with her past and her present;
that is how the final fact at the heart of Flaubert's
subject will be best displayed.

83

Here is the clue, it seems, to his treatment of the theme. It is pictorial, and its object is to make Emma's existence as intelligible and visible as may be. We who read the book are to share her sense of life, till no uncertainty is left in it; we are to see and understand her experience, and to see *her* while she enjoys or endures it; we are to be placed within her world, to get the immediate taste of it, and outside her world as well, to get the full effect, more of it than she herself could see. Flaubert's subject demands no less, if the picture is to be complete. She herself must be known thoroughly—that is his first care; the movement of her mind is to be watched at work in all the ardour and the poverty of her imagination. How she creates her makeshift romances, how she feeds on them, how they fail her—it is all part of the picture. And then there is the dull and limited world in which her appetite is somehow to be satisfied, the small town that shuts her in and cuts her off; this, too, is to be rendered, and in order to make it clearly tell beside the figure of Emma it must be as distinct and individual, as thoroughly characterized as she is. It is more than a setting for Emma and her intrigue; it belongs to the book integrally, much more so than the accidental lovers who fall in Emma's way. They are mere occasions and attractions for her fancy; the town and the *curé* and the apothecary and the other indigenous gossips need a sharper definition. And accordingly Flaubert treats the scenery of his book, Yonville and its

odd types, as intensely as he treats his heroine;
he broods over it with concentration and gives it
all the salience he can. The town with its life is
not behind his heroine, subdued in tone to make
a background; it is *with* her, no less fully to the
front; its value in the picture is as strong as her
own.

Such is the picture that Flaubert's book is to
present. And what, then, of the point of view
towards which it is to be directed? If it is to have
that unity which it needs to produce its right
effect there can be no uncertainty here, no
arbitrary shifting of the place from which an
onlooker faces it. And in the tale of Madame
Bovary the question of the right point of view
might be considerably perplexing. Where is
Flaubert to find his centre of vision?—from what
point, within the book or without, will the unfolding of the subject be commanded most
effectively? The difficulty is this—that while one
aspect of his matter can only be seen from within,
through the eyes of the woman, another must inevitably be seen from without, through nobody's
eyes but the author's own. Part of his subject is
Emma's sense of her world; we must see how it
impresses her and what she makes of it, how it
thwarts her and how her imagination contrives
to get a kind of sustenance out of it. The book
is not really written at all unless it shows her
view of things, as the woman she was, in that
place, in those conditions. For this reason it is
essential to pass into her consciousness, to make

her *subjective*; and Flaubert takes care to do so and to make her so, as soon as she enters the book. But it is also enjoined by the story, as we found, that her place and conditions should be seen for what they are and known as intimately as herself. For this matter Emma's capacity fails.

Her intelligence is much too feeble and fitful to give a sufficient account of her world. The town of Yonville would be very poorly revealed to us if Flaubert had to keep within the measure of *her* perceptions; it would be thin and blank, it would be barely more than a dull background for the beautiful apparition of the men she desires. What were her neighbours to her? They existed in her consciousness only as tiresome interruptions and drawbacks, except now and then when she had occasion to make use of them. But to us, to the onlooker, they belong to her portrait, they represent the dead weight of provincial life which is the outstanding fact in her case. Emma's rudimentary idea of them is entirely inadequate; she has not a vestige of the humour and irony that is needed to give them shape. Moreover they affect her far more forcibly and more variously than she could even suspect; a sharper wit than hers must evidently intervene, helping out the primitive workings of her mind. Her pair of eyes is not enough; the picture beheld through them is a poor thing in itself, for she can see no more than her mind can grasp; and it does her no justice either, since she herself is so largely the creation of her surroundings.

It is a dilemma that appears in any story, wherever the matter to be represented is the experience of a simple soul or a dull intelligence. If it is the experience and the actual taste of it that is to be imparted, the story must be viewed as the poor creature saw it; and yet the poor creature cannot tell the story in full. A shift of the vision is necessary. And in Madame Bovary, it is to be noted, there is no one else within the book who is in a position to take up the tale when Emma fails. There is no other personage upon the scene who sees and understands any more than she; perception and discrimination are not to be found in Yonville at all—it is an essential point. The author's wit, therefore, and none other, must supply what is wanting. This necessity, to a writer of Flaubert's acute sense of effect, is one that demands a good deal of caution. The transition must be made without awkwardness, without calling attention to it. Flaubert is not the kind of story-teller who will leave it undisguised; he will not begin by " going behind " Emma, giving her view, and then openly, confessedly, revert to his own character and use his own standards. There is nothing more disconcerting in a novel than to *see* the writer changing his part in this way—throwing off the character into which he has been projecting himself and taking a new stand outside and away from the story.

Perhaps it is only Thackeray, among the great, who seems to find a positively wilful pleasure in damaging his own story by open maltreatment of this kind; there are times when Thackeray will even boast of his own independence, insisting in so many words on his freedom to say what he pleases about his men and women and to make them behave as he will. But without using Thackeray's licence a novelist may still do his story an ill turn by leaving too naked a contrast between the subjective picture of what passes through Emma's mind—Emma's or Becky's, as it may be—and the objective rendering of what he sees for himself, between the experience that is mirrored in another thought and that which is shaped in his own. When one has lived *into* the experience of somebody in the story and received the full sense of it, to be wrenched out of the story and stationed at a distance is a shock that needs to be softened and muffled in some fashion. Otherwise it may weaken whatever was true and valid in the experience; for here is a new view of it, external and detached, and another mind at work, the author's—and that sense of having shared the life of the person in the story seems suddenly unreal.

Flaubert's way of disguising the inconsistency is not a peculiar art of his own, I dare say. Even in him it was probably quite unconscious, well as he was aware of most of the refinements of his craft; and perhaps it is only a sleight of hand that might come naturally to any good story-teller. But it is interesting to follow Flaubert's method to the very end, for it holds out so consummately; and I think it is possible to define it here. I should say, then, that he deals with the difficulty I have described by keeping Emma always at a certain distance, even when he appears to be entering her mind most freely. He makes her subjective, places us so that we see through her eyes—yes; but he does so with an air of aloofness that forbids us ever to become entirely identified with her. This is how she thought and felt, he seems to say; look and you will understand; such is the soul of this foolish woman. A hint of irony is always perceptible, and it is enough to prevent us from being lost in her consciousness, immersed in it beyond easy recall. The woman's life is very real, perfectly felt; but the reader is made to accept his participation in it as a pleasing experiment, the kind of thing that appeals to a fastidious curiosity—there is no question of its ever being more than this. The *fact* of Emma is taken with entire seriousness, of course; she is there to be studied and explored, and no means of understanding her point of view will be neglected. But her value is another matter; as to that Flaubert never has an instant's illusion, he always knows her to be worthless.

He knows it without asserting it, needless to say; his valuation of her is only implied; it is in his tone—never in his words, which invariably respect her own estimate of herself. His irony, none the less, is close at hand and indispensable; he has a definite use for this resource and he could not forego it. His irony gives him perfect freedom to supersede Emma's limited vision whenever he pleases, to abandon her manner of looking at the world, and to pass immediately to his own more enlightened, more commanding height. Her manner was utterly convincing while she exhibited it; but we always knew that a finer mind was watching her display with a touch of disdain. From time to time it leaves her and begins to create the world of Homard and Binet and Lheureux and the rest, in a fashion far beyond any possible conception of hers. Yet there is no dislocation here, no awkward substitution of one set of values for another; very discreetly the same standard has reigned throughout. That is the way in which Flaubert's impersonality, so called, artfully operates.

And now another difficulty; there is still more that is needed and that is not yet provided for. Emma must be placed in her world and fitted into it securely. Some glimpse of her appearance in the sight of those about her—this, too, we look for, to make the whole account of her compact and complete. Her relation to her husband, for instance, is from her side expressed very clearly in her view of him, which we possess; but there are advantages in seeing it from his side too. What did *he* really think of her, how did she appear to him? Light on this question not only makes a more solid figure of her for the reader, but it also brings her once for all into the company of the people round her, establishes her in the circle of their experience. Emma from within we have seen, and Yonville from the author's point of vantage; and now here is Emma from a point by her very side, when the seeing eye becomes that of her husband. Flaubert manages this ingeniously, making his procedure serve a further purpose at the same time. For he has to remember that his story does not end with the death of Emma; it is rounded off, not by her death, but by her husband's discovery of her long faithlessness, when in the first days of his mourning he lights upon the packet of letters that betrays her. The end of the story is in the final stroke of irony which gives the man this far-reaching glance into the past, and reveals thereby the mental and emotional confusion of his being—since his only response is a sort of stupefied perplexity. Charles must be held in readiness, so to speak, for these last pages; his inner mind, and his point of view, must be created in advance and kept in reserve, so that the force of the climax, when it is reached, may be instantly felt. And so we have the early episodes of Charles's youth and his first marriage, all his history up to the time when he falls in Emma's way; and Flaubert's questionable manner of working round to his subject is explained. Charles will be needed at the end, and Charles is here firmly set on his feet; the impression of Emma on those who encounter her is also needed, and here it is; and the whole book, mainly the affair of Emma herself, is effectively framed in this other affair, that of Charles, in which it opens and closes. Madame Bovary is a well-made book—so we have always been told, and so we find it to be, pulling it to pieces and putting it together again. It never is unrepaying to do so once more.

And it is a book that with its variety of method, and with its careful restriction of that variety to its bare needs, and with its scrupulous use of its resources—it is a book, altogether, that gives a good point of departure for an examination of the methods of fiction. The leading notions that are to be followed are clearly laid down in it, and I shall have nothing more to say that is not in some sense an extension and an amplification of hints to be found in Madame Bovary. For that reason I have lingered in detail over the treatment of a story about which, in other connections, a critic might draw different conclusions. I remember again how Flaubert vilified his subject while he was at work on it; his love of strong colours and flavours was disgusted by the drab prose of such a story—so he thought and said. But as the years went by and he fought his way from one chapter to another, did he begin to feel that it was not much of a subject after all, even of its kind? It is not clear; but after yet another re-reading of the book one wonders afresh. It is not a fertile subject—it is not; it does not strain and struggle for development, it only submits to it. But that aspect is not *my* subject, and Madame Bovary, a beautifully finished piece of work, is for my purpose singularly fertile.

VII

OF the notions on the subject of method that are
suggested by Bovary, the first I shall follow is
one that takes me immediately, without any
doubt whatever, into the world of Thackeray. I
start from that distinction between the "panoramic" and the "scenic" presentation of a story,
which I noted a few pages ago; and to turn towards the panorama, away from the scene, is to
be confronted at once with Vanity Fair, Pendennis, The Newcomes, Esmond, all of them.
Thackeray saw them as broad expanses, stretches
of territory, to be surveyed from edge to edge
with a sweeping glance; he saw them as great
general, typical impressions of life, populated by
a swarm of people whose manners and adventures
crowded into his memory. The landscape lay
before him, his imagination wandered freely
across it, backwards and forwards. The whole of
it was in view at once, a single prospect, out of
which the story of Becky or Pendennis emerged
and grew distinct while he watched. He wrote his
novel with a mind full of a surge and wash of
memories, the tenor of which was somehow to be
conveyed in the outward form of a narrative.
And though his novel complies with that form

more or less, and a number of events are marshalled in order, yet its constant tendency is to escape and evade the restrictions of a scenic method, and to present the story in a continuous flow of leisurely, contemplative reminiscence.

And that is evidently the right way for the kind of story that Thackeray means to create. For what is the point and purpose of Vanity Fair, where is the centre from which it grows? Can it be described as a " plot," a situation, an entanglement, something that raises a question of the issue? Of plots in this sense there are plenty in Vanity Fair, at least there are two; Becky dominates one, Amelia smiles and weeps in the other. They join hands occasionally, but really they have very little to exchange. Becky and her Crawleys, Becky and her meteoric career in Curzon Street, would have been all as they are if Amelia had never been heard of; and Bloomsbury, too, of the Osbornes and the Sedleys, might have had the whole book to itself, for all that Becky essentially matters to it. Side by side they exist, and for Thackeray's purpose neither is more important than the other, neither is in the middle of the book as it stands. Becky seems to be in the middle, certainly, as we think of her; but that is not where Thackeray placed her. He meant Amelia to be no less appealing than Becky is striking; and if Amelia fails and drops into the background, it is not because she plays a subordinate part, but only because she plays it with so much less than Becky's vivid conviction.

They fill the book with incident between the two of them; something is always happening, from the moment when they drive out of Miss Pinkerton's gate at Chiswick till the last word that is told of either. But the book as a whole turns upon nothing that happens, not even upon the catastrophe of Curzon Street; that scene in Becky's drawing-room disposes of *her*, it leaves the rest of the book quite untouched.

Not in any complication of incident, therefore, nor in any single strife of will, is the subject of Vanity Fair to be discerned. It is not here but in the impression of a world, a society, a time— certain manners of life within a few square miles of London, a hundred years ago. Thackeray flings together a crowd of the people he knows so well, and it matters not at all if the tie that holds them to each other is of the slightest; it may easily chance that his good young girl and his young adventuress set out together upon their journey, their paths may even cross from time to time later on. The light link is enough for the unity of his tale, for that unity does not depend on an intricately woven intrigue. It depends in truth upon one fact only, the fact that all his throng of men and women are strongly, picturesquely typical of the world from which they are taken—that all in their different ways can add to the force of its effect. The book is not the story of any of them, it is the story which they unite to tell, a chapter in the notorious career of well-to-do London. Exactly how the

THE CRAFT OF FICTION

various " plots " evolve is not the main matter;
behind them is the presence and the pressure of a
greater interest, the mass of life which Thackeray
packs into his novel. And if that is the meaning
of Vanity Fair, to give the succession of incident
a hard, particular, dramatic relief would be to
obscure it. Becky's valiant struggle in the world
of her ambition might easily be isolated and
turned into a play—no doubt it has been; but
consider how her look, her value, would in that
case be changed. Her story would become a
mere personal affair of her own, the mischance
of a certain woman's enterprise. Given in
Thackeray's way, summarized in his masterly
perspective, it is part of an impression of manners.

Such, I take it, is Thackeray's difference, his
peculiar mark, the distinction of his genius. He
is a painter of life, a novelist whose matter is all
blended and harmonized together—people, action,
background—in a long retrospective vision. Not
for him, on the whole, is the detached action, the
rounded figure, the scenic rendering of a story;
as surely as Dickens tended towards the theatre,
with its clear-cut isolation of events and episodes,
its underlining of the personal and the individual
in men and women, so Thackeray preferred the
manner of musing expatiation, where scene melts
into scene, impressions are foreshortened by
distance, and the backward-ranging thought can
linger and brood as it will. Every novel of his
takes the general form of a discursive soliloquy,
in which he gradually gathers up the long train

of experience that he has in mind. The early
chapters of Esmond or Pendennis, the whole
fragment of Denis Duval, are perfect examples
of Thackeray's way when he is most himself, and
when he is least to be approached by any other
writer of fiction. All that he has to describe, so
it seems, is present to him in the hour of re-
collection; he hangs over it, and his eye is caught
by a point here and there, a child with a book in
a window-seat, the Fotheringay cleaning her old
shoe, the Major at his breakfast in Pall Mall; the
associations broaden away from these glimpses
and are followed hither and thither. But still,
though the fullness of memory is directed into a
consecutive tale, it is not the narrative, not its
order and movement, that chiefly holds either
Thackeray's attention or ours who read; the
narrative is steeped in the suffusion of the general
tone, the sensation of the place and the life that
he is recalling, and it is out of this effect, insensibly
changing and developing, that the novel is
created.

For a nearer sight of it I go back to Vanity
Fair. The chapters that are concerned with
Becky's determined siege of London—" How to
live well on nothing a year "—are exactly to the
point; the wonderful things that Thackeray
could do, the odd lapse of his power when he had
to go beyond his particular province, both are
here written large. Every one remembers the
chapters and their place in the book. Becky,
resolutely shaking off old difficulties for the

moment, installs herself with her husband in the heart of the world she means to conquer; she all but succeeds, she just fails. Her campaign and its untimely end are to be pictured; it is an interlude to be filled with stir and glitter, with the sense of the passage of a certain time, above all with intimations of insecurity and precarious fortune; and it is to lead (this it must do) to a scene of final and decisive climax. Such is the effect to be drawn from the matter that Thackeray has stored up—the whole hierarchy of the Crawleys, Steyne, Gaunt House, always with Becky in the midst and to the fore. Up to a point it is precisely the kind of juncture in which Thackeray's art delights. There is abundance of vivid stuff, and the picture to be made of it is highly functional in the book. It is not merely a preparation for a story to follow; it is itself the story, a most important part of it. The chapters representing Becky's manner of life in Curzon Street make the hinge of her career; she approaches her turning-point at the beginning of them, she is past it at the end. Functional, therefore, they are to the last degree; but up to the very climax, or the verge of it, there is no need for a set scene of dramatic particularity. An impression is to be created, growing and growing; and it can well be created in the loose panoramic style which is Thackeray's paramount arm. A general view, once more, a summary of Becky's course of action, a long look at her conditions, a participation in her gathering difficulties—that is the nature and the task of these chapters, that is what Thackeray proceeds to give us.

He sets about it with a beautiful ease of assurance. From his height he looks forth, takes in the effect with his sweeping vision, possesses himself of the gradation of its tone; then, stooping nearer he seizes the detail that renders it. But the sense of the broad survey is first in his thought. When he reflects upon Becky's life in London and all that came of her attempt to establish herself there, he is soon assailed by a score of definite recollections, tell-tale incidents, scraps of talk that show how things were going with her; but these, it would seem, arise by the way, they spring up in his mind as he reviews the past. They illustrate what he has to say, and he takes advantage of them. He brushes past them, however, without much delaying or particularizing; a hint, a moment, a glance suffices for the contribution that some event or colloquy is to make to the picture. Note, for example, how unceremoniously, again and again, and with how little thought of disposing a deliberate scene, he drifts into his account of something that Becky said or did; she begins to talk, you find there is some one else in the room, you find they are in a certain room at a certain hour; definition emerges unawares in a brooding memory. Briefly, to all appearance quite casually, the little incident shows itself and vanishes; there is a pause to watch and listen, and then the stream sets forward again, by so much enriched and reinforced. Or in a heightened mood, as in the picture of the midnight flurry and alarm of the great desolate house, when old Pitt Crawley is suddenly struck down, still it is as though Thackeray circled about the thought of the time and place, offering swift and piercing glimpses of it, giving no continuous and dramatic display of a constituted scene.

That foreshortening and generalizing, that fusion of detail, that subordination of the instance and the occasion to the broad effect, are the elements of the pictorial art in which Thackeray is so great a master. So long as it is a matter of sketching a train of life in broad free strokes, the poise and swing of his style are beyond praise. And its perfection is all the more notable that it stands in such contrast with the curious drop and uncertainty of his skill, so soon as there is something more, something different to be done. For Becky's dubious adventure has its climax, it tends towards a conclusion, and the final scene cannot be recalled and summarized in his indirect, reminiscential manner. It must be placed immediately before us, the collapse of Becky's plotting and scheming must be enacted in full view, if it is to have its proper emphasis and rightly round off her career. Hitherto we have been listening to Thackeray, on the whole, while he talked about Becky—talked with such extraordinary brilliance that he evoked her in all her ways and made us see her with his eyes; but now it is time to see her with our own, his lively interpretation of her will serve no longer. Does Becky fail in the end? After all that we have heard of her struggle it has become the great question, and the force of the answer will be impaired if it is not given with the best possible warrant. The best possible, better even than Thackeray's wonderful account of her, will be the plain and immediate *performance* of the answer, its embodiment in a scene that shall pass directly in front of us. The method that was not demanded by the preceding phases of the tale is here absolutely prescribed. Becky, Rawdon, Steyne, must now take the matter into their own hands and show themselves without any other intervention. Hitherto, practically throughout, they have been the creatures of Thackeray's thought, they have been openly and confessedly the figures of *his* vision. Now they must come forward, declare themselves, and be seen for what they are.

And accordingly they do come forward and are seen in a famous passage. Rawdon makes his unexpected return home from prison, and Becky's unfortunate disaster overtakes her, so to say, in our very presence. Perhaps I may seem to exaggerate the change of method which I note at this point; but does it not appear to any one, glancing back at his recollection of the book, that this particular scene is defined and relieved and lighted differently, somehow, from the stream of impressions in which it is set? A space is cleared for it, the stage is swept. This is now no retrospective vision, shared with Thackeray; it is a piece of present action with which we are confronted. It is strictly dramatic, and I suppose it is good drama of its kind. But there is more to be said of it than this—more to be said, even when it has been admitted to be drama of rather a high-pitched, theatrical strain. The foot-lights, it is probably agreed, seem suddenly to flare before Becky and Rawdon, after the clear daylight that reigned in Thackeray's description of them; they appear upon the scene, as they should, but it must be owned that the scene has an artificial look, by comparison with the flowing spontaneity of all that has gone before. And this it is exactly that shows how and where Thackeray's skill betrays him. He is not (like Dickens) naturally inclined to the theatre, the melodramatic has no fatal attraction for him; so that if he is theatrical here, it is not because he inevitably would be, given his chance. It is rather because he must, at all costs, make this climax of his story conclusively *tell*; and in order to do so he is forced to use devices of some crudity—for him they are crude—because his climax, his *scène à faire*, has been insufficiently prepared for. Becky, Rawdon, Steyne, in all this matter that has been leading up to the scene, have scarcely before been rendered in these immediate terms; and now that they appear on their own account they can only make a sure and pronounced effect by perceptibly forcing their note. A little too much is expected

THE CRAFT OF FICTION

of them, and they must make an unnatural effort
to meet it.

My instance is a small one, no doubt, to be
pressed so far; in lingering over these shades of
treatment a critic, it may be thought, loses sight
of the book itself. But I am not trying, of course,
to criticize Vanity Fair; I am looking for certain
details of method, and the small instance is
surely illuminating. It shows how little Thackeray's fashion of handling a novel allowed for the
big dramatic scene, when at length it had to be
faced—how he neglected it in advance, how he
refused it till the last possible moment. It is as
though he never quite trusted his men and women
when he had to place things entirely in their care,
standing aside to let them act; he wanted to
intervene continually, he hesitated to leave them
alone save for a brief and belated half-hour. It
was perverse of him, because the men and women
would have acquitted themselves so strikingly
with a better chance; he gave them life and
vigour enough for much more independence than
they ever enjoyed. The culmination of Becky's
adventure offered a clear opening for full dramatic
effect, if he had chosen to take advantage of it.
He had steadily piled up his impression, carefully
brought all the sense of the situation to converge
upon a single point; everything was ready for
the great scene of Becky's triumph in the face of
the world, one memorable night of a party at
Gaunt House. It is incredible that he should let
the opportunity slip. There was a chance of a

straight, unhampered view of the whole meaning of his matter; nothing was needed but to allow the scene to show itself, fairly and squarely. All its force would have been lent to the disaster that follows; the dismay, the disillusion, the snarl of anger and defiance, all would have been made beforehand. By so much would the effect of the impending scene, the scene of catastrophe, have been strengthened. There would have been no necessity for the sudden heightening of the pitch, the thickening of the colour, the incongruous and theatrical tone.

Yet the chance is missed, the triumphal evening passes in a confused haze that leaves the situation exactly where it was before. The episode is only a repetition of the kind of thing that has happened already. There are echoes of festive sound and a rumour of Becky's brilliance; but the significant look that the actual facts might have worn and must have betrayed, the look that by this time Thackeray has so fully instructed his reader to catch—this is not disclosed after all. There is still nothing here but Thackeray's amusing, irrepressible conversation *about* the scene; he cannot make up his mind to clear a space before it and give the situation the free field it cries out for. And if it is asked what kind of clarity I mean, I need only recall another page, close by, which shows it perfectly. Becky had made an earlier appearance at Gaunt House; she had dined there, near the beginning of her social career, and had found herself in a difficulty;

there came a moment when she had to face the frigid hostility of the noble ladies of the party, alone with them in the drawing-room, and her assurance failed. In the little scene that ensues the charming veil of Thackeray's talk is suddenly raised; there is Becky seated at the piano, Lady Steyne listening in a dream of old memories, the other women chattering at a distance, when the jarring doors are thrown open and the men return. It is all over in half a page, but in that glimpse the story is lifted forward dramatically; ocular proof, as it were, is added to Thackeray's account of Becky's doubtful and delicate position. As a matter of curiosity I mention the one moment in the later episode, the evening of those strangely ineffective charades at Gaunt House, which appears to me to open the same kind of rift in the haze; it is a single glimpse of Steyne, applauding Becky's triumph. He is immediately there, an actor in the show, alive and expressive, but he is alone; none of the others so emerges, even Becky is only a luminous spot in the dimness. As for the relation of the three, Steyne, Becky, and her husband, which is on the point of becoming so important, there is nothing to be seen of it.

Right and left in the novels of Thackeray one may gather instances of the same kind—the piercing and momentary shaft of direct vision, the big scene approached and then refused. It is easy to find another in Vanity Fair. Who but Thackeray could have borne to use the famous matter of the Waterloo ball, a wonderful gift for a novelist to find in his path, only to waste it, to dissipate its effect, to get no real contribution from it after all? In the queer, haphazard, polyglot interlude that precedes it Thackeray is, of course, entirely at home; there it is a question of the picture-making he delights in, the large impression of things in general, the evocation of daily life; Brussels in its talkative suspense, waiting for the sound of the guns, feeding on rumour, comes crowding into the chapter. And then the great occasion that should have crowned it, into which the story naturally and logically passes—for again the scene is not a decorative patch, the story needs it—the Waterloo ball is nothing, leaves no image, constitutes no effect whatever; the reader, looking back on the book, might be quite uncertain whether he had been there or not. Nobody could forget the sight of Lady Bareacres, sitting under the *porte cochère* in her horseless carriage—of good Mrs. O'Dowd, rising in the dawn to equip her warrior for battle —of George Osborne, dead on the field; but these are Thackeray's flashes of revelation, straight and sure, and they are all the drama, strictly speaking, that he extorts from his material. The rest is picture, stirringly, vivaciously reflected in his unfailing memory—with the dramatic occasion to which it tends, the historic affair of the "revelry by night," neglected and lost.

There is scarcely need for more illustration

of my point, but it is tempting to look further. In all these well-remembered books Thackeray, in an expansive mood, opens his mind and talks it out on the subject of some big, loosely-knit company of men and women. He remembers, as we all remember, with a strong sense of the tone and air of an old experience, and a sharp re-collection of moments that happened for some reason to be salient, significant, peculiarly keen or curious. Ethel Newcome, when she comes riding into the garden in the early morning, full of the news of her wonderful discovery, the letter shut in the old book; Blanche Amory, when she is caught out in her faithlessness, warbling to the new swain at the piano and whipping her hand-kerchief over his jewel-case as the old one enters; Madam Esmond, on her balcony, defying the mob with " Britons, strike home "; old Sir Pitt, toasting his rasher in the company of the char-woman: I name them at random, they are all instances of the way in which the glance of memory falls on the particular moment, the aspect that hardens and crystallizes an impression. Thackeray has these flashes in profusion; they break out unforgettably as we think of his books. The most exquisite of all, perhaps, is in Esmond, that sight of the dusky choir of Winchester Cathedral, the shine of the candle-light, the clear faces of Rachel and her son as they appear to the returned wanderer. We no longer listen to a story, no longer see the past in a sympathetic imagination; this is a higher power of intensity,

a fragment of the past made present and actual.
But with Thackeray it is always a fragment,
never to any real purpose a deliberate and
continuous enactment.

For continuity he always recurs to his pictorial
summary. The Newcomes alone would give a
dozen examples of this side of his genius—in the
pages that recall the lean dignity of the refugees
from revolutionary Paris, or the pious opulence
of Clapham, or the rustle of fashion round the
Mayfair chapel, or the chatter and scandal of
Baden-Baden, or the squalid pretensions of
English life at Boulogne. I need not lengthen the
list; these evocations follow one upon another,
and as quickly as Thackeray passes into a new
circle he makes us feel and know what it was like
to live there and belong to it. The typical look
of the place is in his mind, the sense of its habitual
life, the savour of the hours that lapse there.
But Esmond again has the last word; the early
chapters of the old days at Castlewood show a
subtlety of effect that is peculiar and rare. It is
more than a picture of a place and an impression
of romance, it is more than the portrait of a child;
besides all this it is the most masterly of " time-
pictures," if that is a word that will serve. The
effect I am thinking of is different from that of
which I spoke in the matter of Tolstoy's great
cycles of action; there we saw the march of time
recording itself, affirming its ceaseless movement,
in the lives of certain people. This of Thackeray's
is not like that; time, at Castlewood, is not move-

ment, it is tranquillity—time that stands still, as we say, only deepening as the years go. It cannot therefore be shown as a sequence; and Thackeray roams to and fro in his narrative, caring little for the connected order of events if he can give the sensation of time, deep and soft and abundant, by delaying and returning at ease over this tract of the past. It would be possible, I think, to say very precisely where and how the effect is made—by what leisurely play with the chronology of the story, apparently careless and unmethodical, or by what shifting of the focus, so that the house of Castlewood is now a far-away memory and now a close, benevolent presence. Time, at any rate, is stored up in the description of the child's life there, quiet layers of time in which the recorded incidents sink deep.

VIII

In dealing with the method that I find peculiarly characteristic of Thackeray, the " panoramic " method, I have spoken of it also as " pictorial "; and it will be noticed that I have thus arrived at another distinction which I touched upon in connection with Bovary. Picture and drama— this is an antithesis which continually appears in a novel, and I shall have much to say of it. And first of the names which I give to these contrasted manners of treatment—I do not know that they are the best names, but they express the main point of difference, and they also have this advantage, that they *have* been used technically in the criticism of fiction, with specific meaning. In writing about novels one is so rarely handling words that have ever been given close definition (with regard to the art of fiction, I mean) that it is natural to grasp at any which have chanced to be selected and strictly applied by a critic of authority. Picture and drama, therefore, I use because Henry James used them in discussing his own novels, when he reviewed them all in his later years; but I use them, I must add, in a rather more extended sense than he did. Anybody who knows the critical prefaces of his books will remember how picture and drama, to him, re-

presented the twofold manner towards which he
tended in his last novels, composed as they are
in a regular alternation of dramatic dialogue and
pictorial description. But *his* pictorial description
was of a very special kind; and when the subject
of criticism is fiction generally, not his alone,
picture will take a wider meaning, as opposed to
drama. It will be found to cover the panoramic
manner of Thackeray.

It is a question, I said, of the reader's relation
to the writer; in one case the reader faces towards
the story-teller and listens to him, in the other
he turns towards the story and watches it. In
the drama of the stage, in the acted play, the
spectator evidently has no direct concern with
the author at all, while the action is proceeding.
The author places their parts in the mouths of the
players, leaves them to make their own impression,
leaves *us*, the audience, to make what we can of
it. The motion of life is before us, the recording,
registering mind of the author is eliminated.
That is drama; and when we think of the story-
teller as opposed to the dramatist, it is obvious
that in the full sense of the word there is no such
thing as drama in a novel. The novelist may give
the very words that were spoken by his characters,
the dialogue, but of course he must interpose
on his own account to let us know how the people
appeared, and where they were, and what they
were doing. If he offers nothing but the bare
dialogue, he is writing a kind of play; just as a
dramatist, amplifying his play with " stage-

111

directions " and putting it forth to be read in a book, has really written a kind of novel. But the difference between the story-teller and the playwright is not my affair; and a new contrast, within the limits of the art of fiction, is apparent when we speak of the novel by itself—a contrast of two methods, to one of which it is reasonable to give the name of drama.

I do not say that a clear line can be drawn between them; criticism does not hope to be mathematically exact. But everybody sees the diversity between the talkative, confidential manner of Thackeray and the severe, discreet, anonymous manner—of whom shall I say?—of Maupassant, for a good example, in many of his stories. It is not only the difference between the personal qualities of the two men, which indeed are also as far apart as the house of Castlewood and the Maison Tellier; it is not the difference between the kinds of story they chose to tell. They approached a story from opposite sides, and thought of it, consequently, in images that had nothing in common: not always, I dare say, but on the whole and characteristically they did so. Maupassant's idea of a story (and not peculiarly Maupassant's, of course, but his name is convenient) would suggest an object that you fashioned and abandoned to the reader, turning away and leaving him alone with it; Thackeray's would be more like the idea of a long and sociable interview with the reader, a companion with whom he must establish definite terms. Enough, the contrast is very familiar. But these are images; how is the difference shown in their written books, in Esmond and La Maison Tellier? Both, it is true, represent a picture that was in the author's mind; but the story passes into Thackeray's book as a picture still, and passes into Maupassant's as something else—I call it drama.

In Maupassant's drama we are close to the facts, against them and amongst them. He relates his story as though he had caught it in the act and were mentioning the details as they passed. There seems to be no particular process at work in his mind, so little that the figure of Maupassant, the showman, is overlooked and forgotten as we follow the direction of his eyes. The scene he evokes is contemporaneous, and there it is, we can see it as well as he can. Certainly he is " telling " us things, but they are things so immediate, so perceptible, that the machinery of his telling, by which they reach us, is unnoticed; the story appears to tell itself. Critically, of course, we know how far that is from being the case, we know with what judicious thought the showman is selecting the points of the scene upon which he touches. But the *effect* is that he is not there at all, because he is doing nothing that ostensibly requires any judgement, nothing that reminds us of his presence. He is behind us, out of sight, out of mind; the story occupies us, the moving scene, and nothing else.

But Thackeray—in *his* story we need him all the time and can never forget him. He it is who must assemble and arrange his large chronicle, piecing it together out of his experience. Becky's mode of life, in his story, is a matter of many details picked up on many occasions, and the power that collects them, the mind that contains them, is always and openly Thackeray's; it could not be otherwise. It is no question, for most of the time, of watching a scene at close quarters, where the simple, literal detail, such as anybody might see for himself, would be sufficient. A stretch of time is to be shown in perspective, at a distance; the story-teller must be at hand to work it into a single impression. And thus the general panorama, such as Thackeray displays, becomes the representation of the author's experience, and the author becomes a personal entity, about whom we may begin to ask questions. Thackeray *cannot* be the nameless abstraction that the dramatist (whether in the drama of the stage or in that of the novel) is naturally. I know that Thackeray, so far from trying to conceal himself, comes forward and attracts attention and nudges the reader a great deal more than he need; he likes the personal relation with the reader and insists on it. But do what he might to disguise it, so long as he is ranging over his story at a height, chronicling, summarizing, foreshortening, he *must* be present to the reader as a narrator and a showman. It is only when he descends and approaches a certain occasion and sets a scene with due circumspection—rarely and a trifle awkwardly, as we saw—that he can for the time being efface the thought of his active part in the affair.

So much of a novel, therefore, as is not dramatic enactment, not *scenic*, inclines always to picture, to the reflection of somebody's mind. Confronted with a scene—like Becky's great scene, once more —we forget that other mind; but as soon as the story goes off again into narrative a question at once arises. *Who* is disposing the scattered facts, whose is this new point of view? It is the omniscient author, and the point of view is his— such would be the common answer, and it is the answer we get in Vanity Fair. By convention the author is allowed his universal knowledge of the story and the people in it. But still it is a con- vention, and a prudent novelist does not strain it unnecessarily. Thackeray in Vanity Fair is not at all prudent; his method, so seldom strictly dramatic, is one that of its nature is apt to force this question of the narrator's authority, and he goes out of his way to emphasize the question still further. He flourishes the fact that the point of view is his own, not to be confounded with that of anybody in the book. And so his book, as one may say, is not complete in itself, not really self- contained; it does not meet and satisfy all the issues it suggests. Over the whole of one side of it there is an inconclusive look, something that draws the eye away from the book itself, into space. It is the question of the narrator's relation to the story.

However unconsciously—and I dare say the

recognition is usually unconscious—the novelist is alive to this difficulty, no doubt; for we may see him, we presently shall, taking various steps to circumvent it. There is felt to be an unsatisfactory want of finish in leaving a question hanging out of the book, like a loose end, without some kind of attempt to pull it back and make it part of an integral design. After all, the book is torn away from its author and given out to the world; the author is no longer a wandering *jongleur* who enters the hall and utters his book to the company assembled, retaining his book as his own inalienable possession, himself and his actual presence and his real voice indivisibly a part of it. The book that we read has no such support; it must bring its own recognisances. And in the fictitious picture of life the effect of validity is all in all and there can be no appeal to an external authority; and so there is an inherent weakness in it if the mind that knows the story and the eye that sees it remain unaccountable. At any moment they may be questioned, and the only way to silence the question is somehow to make the mind and the eye objective, to make them facts in the story. When the point of view is definitely included in the book, when it can be recognized and verified there, then every side of the book is equally wrought and fashioned. Otherwise it may seem like a thing meant to stand against a wall, with one side left in the rough; and there is no wall for a novel to stand against.

THE CRAFT OF FICTION

That this is not a fanciful objection to a pictorial book like Vanity Fair, where the point of
view is *not* accounted for, is proved, I think, by
the different means that a novelist will adopt to
authenticate his story—to dramatize the seeing
eye, as I should prefer to put it. These I shall try
to deal with in what seems to be their logical
order; illuminating examples of any of them are
not wanting. I do not suggest that if I were criticizing Vanity Fair I should think twice about
this aspect of it; to do so would be very futile
criticism of such a book, such a store of life. But
then I am not considering it as Vanity Fair, I
am considering it as a dominant case of pictorial
fiction; and here is the characteristic danger of
the method, and a danger which all who practise
the method are not likely to encounter and over-
ride with the genius of Thackeray. And even
Thackeray—he chose to encounter it once again,
it is true, in Pendennis, but only once and no
more, and after that he took his own precautions,
and evidently found that he could move the more
freely for doing so.

But to revert yet again for a moment to Bovary—which seemed on scrutiny to be more of a
picture than a drama—I think it is clear how
Flaubert avoided the necessity of installing
himself avowedly as the narrator, in the sight of
the reader. I mentioned how he constantly
blends his acuter vision with that of Emma, so
that the weakness of her gift of experience is
helped out; and the help is mutual, for on the

other hand her vision is always active as far as it goes, and Flaubert's intervention is so unobtrusive that her point of view seems to govern the story more than it does really. And therefore, though the book is largely a picture, a review of many details and occasions, the question of the narrator is never insistent. The landscape that Thackeray controls is so much wider and fuller that even with all the tact of Flaubert—and little he has of it—he could scarcely follow Flaubert's example. His book is not a portrait of character but a panorama of manners, and there is no disguising the need of some detached spectator, who looks on from without.

It is the method of picture-making that enables the novelist to cover his great spaces of life and quantities of experience, so much greater than any that can be brought within the acts of a play. As for intensity of life, that is another matter; there, as we have seen, the novelist has recourse to his other arm, the one that corresponds with the single arm of the dramatist. Inevitably, as the plot thickens and the climax approaches—inevitably, wherever an impression is to be emphasized and driven home—narration gives place to enactment, the train of events to the particular episode, the broad picture to the dramatic scene. But the limitation of drama is as obvious as its peculiar power. It is clear that if we wish to see an abundance and multitude of life we shall find it more readily and more summarily by looking for an hour into a memory, a consciousness, than by merely watching the present events of an hour, however crowded. Much may happen in that time, but in extent it will be nothing to the regions thrown open by the other method. A novelist, with a large and discursive subject before him, could not hope to show it all dramatically; much of it, perhaps the greater part, must be so marshalled that it may be swept by a travelling glance. Thackeray shows how it is done and how a vista of many facts can be made to fall into line; but he shows, too, how it needs a mind to create that vista, and how the creative mind becomes more and more perceptible, more visibly active, as the prospect widens.

Most novelists, I think, seem to betray, like Thackeray, a preference for one method or the other, for picture or for drama; one sees in a moment how Fielding, Balzac, George Eliot, incline to the first, in their diverse manners, and Tolstoy (certainly Tolstoy, in spite of his big range) or Dostoevsky to the second, the scenic way. But of course every novelist uses both, and the quality of a novelist appears very clearly in his management of the two, how he guides the story into the scene, how he picks it out of the scene, a richer and fuller story than it was before, and proceeds with his narrative. On the whole, no doubt, the possibilities of the scene are greatly abused in fiction, in the daily and familiar novel. They are doubly abused; for the treatment of the scene is neglected, and yet it recurs again and again, much too often, and its value is wasted.

It has to be remembered that drama is the novelist's highest light, like the white paper or white paint of a draughtsman; to use it prodigally where it is not needed is to lessen its force where it is essential. And so the economical procedure would be to hoard it rather, reserving it for important occasions—as in Bovary, sure enough.

But before I deal with the question of the novelist's drama I would follow out the whole argument that is suggested by his reflected picture of life. This, after all, is the method which is his very own, which he commands as a story-teller pure and simple. And for a beginning I have tried to indicate its prime disadvantage, consisting of the fact that in its plain form it drags in the omniscient author and may make him exceedingly conspicuous. Why is this a disadvantage, is it asked? It is none, of course, if the author has the power to make us admire and welcome the apparition, or if his picture is so dazzling that a theoretic defect in it is forgotten. But a novel in which either of these feats is accomplished proves only the charm or genius of the author; charm and genius do what they will, there is nothing new in that. And I believe that the defect, even though at first sight it may seem a trifle, is apt to become more and more troublesome in a book as the book is re-read. It makes for a kind of thinness in the general impression, wherever the personal force of the writer is not remarkable. I should say that it

may often contribute towards an air of ineffect-
iveness in a story, which it might otherwise be
difficult to explain.

The fiction of Turgenev is on the whole a case
in point, to my mind. Turgenev was never shy
of appearing in his pages as the reflective story-
teller, imparting the fruits of his observation to
the reader. He will watch a character, let us say,
cross a field and enter a wood and sit down under
a tree; good, it is an opportunity for gaining a
first impression of the man or woman, it is a
little scene, and Turgenev's touch is quick and
light. But then with perfect candour he will show
his hand; he will draw the reader aside and pour
into his ear a flow of information about the man
or woman, information that openly comes straight
from Turgenev himself, in good pictorial form,
no doubt, but information which will never have
its due weight with the reader, because it reposes
upon nothing that he can test for himself. Who
and what is this communicative participator in
the business, this vocal author? He does not
belong to the book, and his voice has not that
compelling tone and tune of its own (as Thackeray's had) which makes a reader enjoy hearing
it for its own sake. This is a small matter, I
admit, but Turgenev extends it and pursues the
same kind of course in more important affairs.
He remains the observant narrator, to whom we
are indebted for a share in his experience. The
result is surely that his picture of life has less
authority than its highly finished design would

seem to warrant. It is evidently not a picture in
which the deeps of character are sounded, and in
which the heights of passion are touched, and in
which a great breadth of the human world is
contained; it is not a picture of such dimensions.
But it has so much neat and just and even
exquisite work in it that it might seem final of
its kind, completely effective in what it attempts;
and it falls short of this, I should say, and there
is something in that constant sense of Turgenev
at one's elbow, *proffering* the little picture, that
may very well damage it. The thing ought to
stand out by itself; it could easily be made to so
so. But Turgenev was unsuspecting; he had not
taken to heart the full importance of dramatizing
the point of view—perhaps it was that.

The narrative, then, the chronicle, the summary,
which must represent the story-teller's ordered
and arranged experience, and which must accordingly be of the nature of a picture, is to be
strengthened, is to be raised to a power approach-
ing that of drama, where the intervention of the
story-teller is no longer felt. The freedom which
the pictorial method gives to the novelist is
unknown to the playwright; but that freedom
has to be paid for by some loss of intensity, and
the question is how to pay as little as possible.
In the end, as I think it may be shown, the loss
is made good and there is nothing to pay at all,
so far may the dramatizing process be followed.
Method, I have said, can be imposed upon method,
one kind upon another; and in analyzing the

manner of certain novelists one discovers how
ingeniously they will correct the weakness of one
method by the force of another and retain the
advantages of both. It is rather a complicated
story, but the beginning is clear enough, and the
direction which it is to take is also clear. Everything in the novel, not only the scenic episodes
but all the rest, is to be in some sense dramatized;
that is where the argument tends. As for the
beginning of it, the first obvious step, the example
of Thackeray is at hand and it could not be
bettered. I turn to Esmond.

IX

THE novelist, I am supposing, is faced with a situation in his story where for some good reason more is needed than the simple impression which the reader might have formed for himself, had he been present and using his eyes on the spot. It is a case for a general account of many things; or it is a case for a certain view of the facts, based on inner knowledge, to be presented to the reader. Thackeray, for example, has to open his mind on the subject of Becky's ambitions or Amelia's regrets; it would take too long, perhaps it would be impossible, to set them acting their emotions in a form that would tell the reader the whole tale; their creator must elucidate the matter. He cannot forget, however, that this report of their emotions is a subjective affair of his own; it relies upon his memory of Becky's or Amelia's plight, his insight into the workings of their thought, his sense of past action. All this is vivid enough to the author, who has seen and known, but the reader stands at a further remove.

It would be different if this consciousness of the past, the mind which holds the memory, should itself become for the reader a directly perceptible fact. The author must supply his view, but he might treat his view as though it were in its turn a piece of action. It *is* a piece of action, or of activity, when he calls up these old recollections; and why should not that effort be given the value of a sort of drama on its own account? It would then be like a play within a play; the outer framework at least—consisting of the reflective mind—would be immediately in front of the reader; and its relation to the thing framed, the projected vision, would explain itself. So long as the recorder stands outside and away from his book, as Thackeray stands outside Vanity Fair, a potential value is wasted; the activity that is proceeding in his mind is not in itself an element in the effect of the book, as it might be. And if it were thus drawn into the book it would do double duty; it would authenticate and so enhance the picture; it would add a new and independent interest as well. It seems that there is everything to be said for making a drama of the narrator himself.

And so Thackeray evidently felt, for in all his later work he refused to remain the unaccountable seer from without. He did not carry the dramatizing process very far, indeed, and it may be thought that the change in his method does not amount to much. In The Newcomes and its successors the old Thackerayan display seems essentially the same as ever, still the familiar, easy-going, intimate outpouring, with all the well-known inflexions of Thackeray's voice and the humours of his temperament; certainly

Pendennis and Esmond and George Warrington and Thackeray have all of them exactly the same conception of the art of story-telling, they all command the same perfection of luminous style. And not only does Thackeray stop short at an early stage of the process I am considering, but it must be owned that he uses the device of the narrator " in character " very loosely and casually, as soon as it might be troublesome to use it with care. But still he takes the step, and he picks up the loose end I spoke of, and he packs it into his book; and thenceforward we see precisely how the narrator stands towards the story he unfolds. It is the first step in the dramatization of picture.

A very simple and obvious step too, it will be said, the natural device of the story-teller for giving his tale a look of truth. It is so indeed; but the interest of the matter lies in recognizing exactly what it is that is gained, what it is that makes that look. Esmond tells the story quite as Thackeray would; it all comes streaming out as a pictorial evocation of old times; there is just as little that is strictly dramatic in it as there is in Vanity Fair. Rarely, very rarely indeed, is there anything that could be called a scene; there is a long impression that creeps forward and forward, as Esmond retraces his life, with those piercing moments of vision which we remember so well. But to the other people in the book it makes all the difference that the narrator is among them. Now, when Beatrix appears, we know who it is that so sees her, and we know where the seer is placed; his line of sight, striking across the book, from him the seer to her the seen, is measurable, its angle is shown; it gives to Beatrix a new dimension and a sharper relief. Can you remember any moment in Vanity Fair when you beheld Becky as again and again you behold Beatrix, catching the very slant of the light on her face? Becky never suddenly flowered out against her background in that way; some want of solidity and of objectivity there still is in Becky, and there must be, because she is regarded from anywhere, from nowhere, from somewhere in the surrounding void. Thackeray's language about her does not carry the same weight as Esmond's about Beatrix, because nobody knows where Thackeray is, or what his relation may be to Becky.

This, then, is the readiest means of dramatically heightening a reported impression, this device of telling the story in the first person, in the person of somebody in the book; and large in our fiction the first person accordingly bulks. The characterized " I " is substituted for the loose and general " I " of the author; the loss of freedom is more than repaid by the more salient effect of the picture. Precision, individuality is given to it by this pair of eyes, known and named, through which the reader sees it; instead of drifting in space above the spectacle he keeps his allotted station and contemplates a delimited field of vision. There is much benefit in the sense that the picture has now a definite edge; its value is brought out to the best advantage when its bounding line is thus emphasized. Moreover, it is not only the field of vision that is determined by the use of the first person, it is also the quality of the tone. When we are shown what Esmond sees, and nothing else, there is first of all the comfortable assurance of the point of view, and then there is the personal colour which he throws over his account, so that it gains another kind of distinction. It does not matter that Esmond's tone in his story is remarkably like Thackeray's in the stories that *he* tells; in Esmond's case the tone has a meaning in the story, is part of it, whereas in the other case it is related only to Thackeray, and Thackeray is in the void. When Esmond ruminates and reflects, his manner is the expression of a human being there present, to whom it can be referred; when Thackeray does the same, there is no such compactness, and the manner trails away where we cannot follow it. Dramatically it seems clear that the method of Esmond has the advantage over the method of Vanity Fair.

Here are sound reasons, so far as they go, for the use of the first person in the distinctively pictorial book. David Copperfield, for instance —it is essentially a long glance, working steadily over a tract of years, alone of its kind in Dickens's fiction. It was the one book in which he rejected the intrigue of action for the centre of his design —did not reject it altogether, indeed, but accepted

it as incidental only. Always elsewhere it is
his chosen intrigue, his "plot," that makes the
shape of his book. Beginning with a deceptive
air of intending mainly a novel of manners and
humours, as Stevenson once pointed out, in
Bleak House or in Little Dorrit or in Our
Mutual Friend—in his later books generally—he
insinuates a thread of action that gradually twists
more and more of the matter of the book round
itself. The intrigue begins to take the first place,
to dominate and at last to fill the pages. That
was the form, interesting of its kind, and one to
which justice has hardly been done, which he
elaborated and made his own. In Copperfield
for once he took another way entirely. It is the
far stretch of the past which makes the shape of
that book, not any of the knots or networks of
action which it contains. These, instead of controlling the novel, sink into the level of retrospect.
Copperfield has not a few lesser dramas to
represent; but the affair of Steerforth, the affair
of Uriah Heep, to name a pair of them, which
might have developed and taken command of the
scene, fall back into the general picture, becoming
incidents in the long rhythm of Copperfield's
memory. It was a clear case for narration in
person, in character; everything was gained and
nothing lost by leaving it to the man to give his
own impression. Nothing was lost, because the
sole need is for the reader to see what David
sees; it matters little how his mind works, or
what the effect of it all may be upon himself. It

is the story of what happened around him, not within. David offers a pair of eyes and a memory, nothing further is demanded of him.

But now let me take the case of another big novel, where again there is a picture outspread, with episodes of drama that are subordinate to the sweep of the expanse. It is Meredith's story of Harry Richmond, a book in which its author evidently found a demand in some way different from that of the rest of his work; for here again the first person is used by a man who habitually avoided it. In Harry Richmond it seemed to Meredith appropriate, I suppose, because the story has a romantic and heroic temper, the kind of chivalrous fling that sits well on a youth of spirit, telling his own tale. It is natural for the youth to pass easily from one adventure to the next, taking it as it comes; and if Meredith proposes to write a story of loose, generous, informal design he had better place it in the mouth of the adventurer. True that in so far as it is romantic, and a story of youth, and a story in which an air from an age of knight-errantry blows into modern times, so that something like a clash of armour and a splintering of spears seems to mingle with the noises of modern life—true that in so far as it is all this, Harry Richmond is not alone among Meredith's books. The author of Richard Feverel and Evan Harrington and Beauchamp and Lord Ormont was generally a little vague on the question of the century in which his stories were cast. The events may happen in the nineteenth century, they clearly must; and yet the furniture and the machinery and the conventions of the nineteenth century have a way of appearing in Meredith's pages as if they were anachronisms. But that is by the way; Harry Richmond is certainly, on the face of it, a series of adventures loosely connected—connected only by the fact that they befell a particular young man; and so the method of narration should emphasize the link, Meredith may have concluded, and the young man shall speak for himself.

The use of the first person, no doubt, is a source of relief to a novelist in the matter of composition. It composes of its own accord, or so he may feel; for the hero gives the story an indefeasible unity by the mere act of telling it. His career may not seem to hang together logically, artistically; but every part of it is at least united with every part by the coincidence of its all belonging to one man. When he tells it himself, that fact is serviceably to the fore; the first person will draw a rambling, fragmentary tale together and stamp it after a fashion as a single whole. Does anybody dare to suggest that this is a reason for the marked popularity of the method among our novelists? Autobiography—it is a regular literary form, and yet it is one which refuses the recognized principles of literary form; its natural right is to seem wayward and inconsequent; its charm is in the fidelity with which it follows the winding course of the writer's thought, as he muses upon the past, and the writer is not expected to guide his thought in an orderly design, but to let it wander free. Formlessness becomes actually the mark of right form in literature of this class; and a novel presented as fictitious autobiography gets the same advantage. And there the argument brings us back to the old question; fiction must *look* true, and there is no look of truth in inconsequence, and there is no authority at the back of a novel, independent of it, to vouch for the truth of its apparent wilfulness. But it is not worth while to linger here; the use of the first person has other and more interesting snares than this, that it pretends to disguise unmeaning, inexpressive form in a story.

Now with regard to Harry Richmond, ostensibly it *is* rather like a chronicle of romantic adventure—not formless, far from it, but freely flowing as a saga, with its illegitimate dash of blood-royal and its roaring old English squire-archy and its speaking statue and its quest of the princess; it *contains* a saga, and even an exceedingly fantastic one. But Harry Richmond is a deeply compacted book, and mixed with its romance there is a novel of another sort. For the fantasy it is only necessary that Harry himself should give a picture of his experience, of all that he has seen and done; on this side the story is in the succession of rare, strange, poetic events, with the remarkable people concerned in them. But the aim of the book goes far beyond this; it is to give the portrait of Harry Richmond, and that is the real reason why the story is told. All these striking episodes, which Harry is so well placed to describe, are not merely pictures that pass, a story that Meredith sets him to tell because it is of high interest on its own account. Meredith's purpose is that the hero himself shall be in the middle of the book, with all the interest of the story reflected back upon his character, his temper, his growth. The subject is Harry Richmond, a youth of spirit; the subject is *not* the cycle of romance through which he happens to have passed.

In the case of Copperfield, to go back to him, Dickens had exactly the opposite intention. He found his book in the expanse of life which his David had travelled over; Dickens's only care was to represent the wonderful show that filled his hero's memory. The whole phantasmagoria is the subject of the book, a hundred men and women, populating David's past and keeping his pen at full speed in the single-minded effort to portray them. Alone among the assembly David himself is scarcely of the subject at all. He has substance enough, and amply, to be a credible, authoritative reporter—Dickens sees well to that; but he is a shadow compared with Betsy Trotwood and the Micawbers and the Heeps, with all the hundred of them, and there is no call for him to be more. In this respect his story, again, is contrasted with that of Pendennis, which is, or is evidently meant to be in the first place, a portrait

of the young man—or with the story of Tom
Jones perhaps, though in this case more doubt-
fully, for Fielding's shrewd eye was apt to be
drawn away from the young man to the bustle of
life around him. But in Copperfield the design
is very plain and is consistently pursued; it
would be a false patch in the story if at any
point David attracted more attention to himself
than to the people of his vision—he himself, as
a child, being of course one of them, a little
creature that he sees in the distance, but he
himself, in later years, becoming merely the
mirror of his experience, which he not unnaturally
considers worthy of being pictured for its own
sake.

Look back then at Harry Richmond, and it is
obvious that Harry himself is all the subject of
the book, there is no other. His father and his
grandfather, Ottilia and Janet, belong to the
book by reason of him; they stand about him,
conditions of his life, phases of his career, deter-
mining what he is and what he becomes. That
is clearly Meredith's thought in undertaking this
chronicle; he proposes to show how it makes
the history, the moral and emotional history, of
the man through whom it is uttered. Harry's
adventures, ambitions, mistakes, successes, are
the gradual and elaborate expression of him,
complete in the end; they round him into the
figure of the man in whom Meredith saw his book.
The book started from Harry Richmond, the
rest of it is there to display him. A youth of

considerable parts and attractions, and a youth
characteristic of his time and country, and a
youth whose circumstances are such as to give
him very free play and to test and prove him
very effectually—there is the burden of Meredith's saga, as I call it, and he never forgets it,
though sometimes he certainly pushes the brilliant fantasy of the saga beyond his strict needs.
The romance of the blood-royal, for instance—it
would be hard to argue that the book honestly
requires the high colour of that infusion, and all
the pervading thrill that Meredith gets from it;
Richmond Roy is largely gratuitous, a piece of
indulgence on Meredith's part. But that objection is not likely to be pressed very severely, and
anyhow Harry is firmly established in the forefront. He tells his story, he describes the company and the scenes he has lived through; and
all the time it is by them that he is himself
described.

It comes to this, that the picture which Harry
Richmond gives of his career has a function
essentially dramatic; it has a part to perform
in the story, a part it must undertake as a whole,
over and above its pictorial charge. It must do
something as well as be, it must create even while
it is created. In Esmond and in Copperfield it
is otherwise; there the unrolling scene has little or
no part to play, as a scene, over against another
actor; it holds no dialogue, so to speak, sustains
no interchange, or none of principal importance,
with the figure of the narrator. He narrates, he

creates the picture; but for us who look on, reading the book, there is nothing in the picture to make us perpetually turn from it and face towards the man in the foreground, watching for the effect it may produce in him. Attention is all concentrated in the life that he remembers and evokes. He himself, indeed, though the fact of his presence is very clear to us, tends to remain in shadow; it is as though he leant from a window, surveying the world, his figure outlined against the lighted square, his features not very distinctly discerned by the reader within. It is enough that he should make Micawber live again, make Beatrix appear on the staircase of the old house, with her scarlet ribbon and the taper in her hand. *They* owe everything to the presence of the man who calls them back from the past; they receive their being, they do little in return.

This picture, this bright vision, spied through the clever ministration of a narrator, is not enough for Harry Richmond. Here the peopled view, all of it together, is like an actor in a play, and the interlocutor, the protagonist, is the man in the foreground, Harry himself. There is no question of simply seeing through his eyes, sharing his memory, perhaps even a little forgetting him from time to time, when the figured scene is particularly delightful. The thought, the fancy, the emotion of Harry Richmond are the centre of the play; from these to the men and women who shape his fate, from them again to the mind that recalls them, attention passes and

returns; we who look on are continually occupied
with the fact of Harry's consciousness, its
gradual enlargement and enrichment. That is
the process which Ottilia and Janet and the rest
of them are expected to forward, and they
contribute actively. Harry before the quest of
the princess and Harry when it has finally failed
are different beings, so far as a man is changed
by an experience that is absorbed into the whole
of his nature. How is the change effected, what
does it achieve?—the episode, bringing the
change into view, dramatizes it, and the question
is answered. The young knight-errant has run an
eventful course, and he gives his account of it;
but the leading event of his tale is himself. His
account illustrates that event, helps towards the
enactment of it. Pictorial, therefore, in form,
dramatic in function—such was the story that
Meredith elected to tell in the first person.

And in so doing he showed, as it seems to me,
precisely where the defect of the method begins
to be felt. The method has a certain dramatic
energy, we have seen, making a visible fact of
the relation, otherwise unexplained, between the
narrator and the tale. It has this; but for a
subject like Meredith's it is really too little, and
the use of the first person is overtaxed. Does he
contrive to conceal the trouble, does he make us
exceedingly unconscious of it while we read the
book? I have no doubt that he does, with the
humanity and poetry and wisdom that he pours
into it—the novel of which it has been said that

if Shakespeare revisited the globe and asked for a book of our times to read, this would be the volume to offer him, the book more likely than another to convince him at once that literature is still in our midst. There is small doubt that Meredith disguises the trouble, and there is still less that he was quite unaware of it himself. But it is there, and it shows plainly enough in some novels, where a personal narrator is given the same kind of task; and in Meredith's book too, I think, it is not to be missed when one considers what might have been, supposing Meredith had chosen another way. The other way was open; he cannot have noticed it.

The young man Harry—this is the trouble—is only a recorder, a picture-maker, so long as he speaks for himself. He is very well placed for describing his world, which *needs* somebody to describe it; his world is much too big and complex to be shown scenically, in those immediate terms I spoke of just now in connection with Maupassant's story. Scenes of drama there may be from time to time, there are plenty in Meredith's novel; but still on the whole the story must be given as the view of an onlooker, and Harry is clearly the onlooker indicated, the only possible one. That is certain; but then there is laid upon him the task which is not laid, or barely at all, upon Copperfield or Esmond. Before the book is out he must have grown to ten times the weight that we dream of looking for in either of them. He must be distinct to see; *he* cannot remain a dim silhouette against the window, the light must fall full upon his face. How can he manage it? How can he give that sharp impression of himself that he easily gives of his world? It is a query that he is in no position to meet, for the impossible is asked of him. He is expected to lend us his eyes (which he does), and yet at the same time to present himself for us to behold with our own; the subject of his story requires no less.

It is not merely a matter of seeing his personal aspect and address; these are readily given by implication. When we have watched for a while the behaviour of the people round him, and have heard something of his experience and of the way in which he fared in the world, we shall very well know what he was like to meet, what others saw in him. There is no difficulty here. But Harry needs a great deal more substance than this, if his story is to be rightly understood. What it was like to *be* Harry, with all that action and reaction of character and fortune proceeding within him—that is the question, the chief question; and since it is the most important affair in the book, it should obviously be rendered as solidly as possible, by the most emphatic method that the author can command. But Harry, speaking of himself, can only report; he can only recall the past and *tell* us what he was, only *describe* his emotion; and he may describe very vividly, and he does, but it would necessarily be more convincing if we could get behind his description and judge for ourselves. Drama we want, always drama, for the central, essential, paramount affair, whatever it is; Harry's consciousness ought to be dramatized. Something is lost if it is represented solely by his account of it. Meredith may enable Harry to give an account so brilliant that the defect is forgotten; that is not the point. But could he have done more? I think so; only it would have meant the surrender of the method of autobiography.

Here then, I conclude, the dramatizing force of the first person gives out. It is very useful for enhancing the value of a picture, where none but the pictorial method is available, where we are bound to rely upon an intervening story-teller in some guise or other; it is much more satisfactory to know who the story-teller is, and to see him as a part of the story, than to be deflected away from the book by the author, an arbitrary, unmeasurable, unappraisable factor. But when the man in the book is expected to make a picture of himself, a searching and elaborate portrait, then the limit of his capacity is touched and passed; or rather there is a better method, one of finer capacity, then ready to the author's hand, and there is no reason to be content with the hero's mere report. The figure of the story-teller is a dramatic fact in Meredith's book, and that is all to the good; but the story-teller's inner history— it is not clear that we need the intervention of anybody in this matter, and if it might be dramatized, made immediately visible, dramatized it evidently should be. By all means let us have Harry's account if we must have somebody's, but perhaps there is no such need. There seems to be none; it is surely time to take the next step in the process I am trying to track.

X

AND the next step is to lay aside the autobiographic device which the novelist was seen to adopt, a few pages ago, in the interest of drama. When it has served as Dickens and Thackeray made it serve, it seems to have shown the extent of its power; if the picture of a life is to be still further dramatized, other arts must be called into play. I am still assuming that the novel under consideration is one that postulates—as indeed most novels do—a point of view which is not that of the reader; I am supposing that the story requires a seeing eye, in the sense I suggested in speaking of Vanity Fair. If no such selecting, interpreting, composing minister is needed, then we have drama unmixed; and I shall come across an example or so in fiction later on. It is drama unmixed when the reader is squarely in front of the scene, all the time, knowing nothing about the story beyond so much as may be gathered from the aspect of the scene, the look and speech of the people. That does not happen often in fiction, except in short pieces, small *contes*. And still I am concerned with the kind of book that preponderantly needs the seeing eye— the kind of novel that I call distinctively pictorial.

The novelist, therefore, returns to the third

person again, but he returns with a marked difference. He by no means resumes his original part, that of Thackeray in Vanity Fair; for his hero's personal narration he does not substitute his own once more. It is still the man in the book who sees and judges and reflects; all the picture of life is still rendered in the hero's terms. But the difference is that instead of receiving his report we now see him in the act of judging and reflecting; his consciousness, no longer a matter of hearsay, a matter for which we must take his word, is now before us in its original agitation. Here is a spectacle for the reader, with no obtrusive interpreter, no transmitter of light, no conductor of meaning. This man's interior life is cast into the world of independent, rounded objects; it is given room to show itself, it appears, it *acts*. A distinction is made between the scene which the man surveys, and the energy within him which converts it all into the stuff of his own being. The scene, as much as ever, is watched through his eyes; but now there is this other fact, in front of the scene, actually under the hand of the reader. To this fact the value of drama has accrued.

Meredith would have sacrificed nothing, so far as I can see, by proceeding to the further stage in Harry Richmond—unless perhaps the story, told in the third person, might seem to lose some of its airings of romance. On the other hand, the advantage of following the stir of Harry's imagination *while* it is stirring would be great;

143

the effect would be straighter, the impression deeper, the reader would have been nearer to Harry throughout, and more closely implicated in his affair. Think of the young man, for instance, in Dostoevsky's Crime and Punishment—there is a young man whose experience surrounds and presses upon the reader, is felt and tasted and endured by the reader; and any one who has been through the book has truly become Raskolnikov, and knows exactly what it was to be that young man. Drama is there pushed into the theatre of a mind; the play proceeds with the reading of the book, accompanying the eye that falls on it. How could a retrospect in the words of the young man—only of course Dostoevsky had no choice in the matter, such a method was ruled out—but supposing the story had admitted it, how could a retrospect have given Raskolnikov thus bodily into the reader's possession? There could have been no conviction in his own account comparable with the certainty which Dostoevsky has left to us, and left because he neither spoke for himself (as the communicative author) nor allowed Raskolnikov to speak, but uncovered the man's mind and made us look.

It seems, then, to be a principle of the story-teller's art that a personal narrator will do very well and may be extremely helpful, so long as the story is only the reflection of life beyond and outside him; but that as soon as the story begins to find its centre of gravity in his own life, as soon as the main weight of attention is claimed for the speaker rather than for the scene, then his report of himself becomes a matter which might be strengthened, and which should accordingly give way to the stronger method. This I take to be a general principle, and where it appears to be violated a critic would instinctively look for the particular reason which makes it inapplicable to the particular case. No reflection, no picture, where living drama is possible—it is a good rule; do not let the hero come between us and his active mind, do not let the heroine stand in front of her emotions and portray them —unless for cause, for some needful effect that would otherwise be missed. I see the reason and the effect very plainly in Thackeray's Barry Lyndon, to take a casual example, where the point of the whole thing is that the man should give himself away unknowingly; in Jane Eyre, to take another, I see neither—but it is hard to throw such a dry question upon tragic little Jane.

If it should still be doubted, however, whether the right use of autobiography is really so limited, it might be a good answer to point to Henry James's Strether, in The Ambassadors; Strether may stand as a living demonstration of all that autobiography cannot achieve. He is enough to prove finally how far the intricate performance of thought is beyond the power of a man to record in his own language. Nine-tenths of Strether's thought—nine-tenths, that is to say, of the silvery activity which makes him what he is— would be lost but for the fact that its adventures are caught in time, while they are proceeding, and enacted in the book. Pictured by him, as he might himself look back on them, they would drop to the same plane as the rest of the scene, the picture of the other people in the story; his state of mind would figure in his description on the same terms as the world about him, it would simply be a matter for him to describe like another. In the book as it is, Strether personally has nothing to do with the impression that is made by the mazy career of his imagination, he has no hand in the effect it produces. It speaks for itself, it spreads over the scene and colours the world just as it did for Strether. It is immediately in the foreground, and the " seeing eye " to which it is presented is not his, but the reader's own.

No longer a figure that leans and looks out of a window, scanning a stretch of memory—that is not the image suggested by Henry James's book. It is rather as though the reader himself were at the window, and as though the window opened straight into the depths of Strether's conscious existence. The energy of his perception and discrimination is there seen at work. His mind is the mirror of the scene beyond it, and the other people in the book exist only in relation to him; but his mind, his own thought of them, is there absolutely, its restless evolution is in full sight. I do not say that this is a complete account of the principle on which the book is constructed; for indeed the principle goes further, encompassing points of method to be dealt with later. But for the moment let the book stand as the type of the novel in which a mind is dramatized— reflecting the life to which it is exposed, but itself performing its own peculiar and private life. This last, in the case of Strether, involves a gradual, long-drawn change, from the moment when he takes up the charge of rescuing his young friend from the siren of Paris, to the moment when he finds himself wishing that his young friend would refuse to be rescued. Such is the curve in the unexpected adventure of his imagination. It is given as nobody's view—not his own, as it would be if he told the story himself, and not the author's, as it would be if Henry James told the story. The author does not tell the story of Strether's mind; he makes it tell itself, he dramatizes it.

Thus it is that the novelist pushes his responsibility further and further away from himself. The fiction that he devises is ultimately his; but it looks poor and thin if he openly claims it as his, or at any rate it becomes much more substantial as soon as he fathers it upon another. This is not *my* story, says the author; you know nothing of me; it is the story of this man or woman in whose words you have it, and he or she is a person whom you *can* know; and you may see for yourselves how the matter arose, the man and woman being such as they are; it all hangs together, and it makes a solid and significant piece of life. And having said this, the author has only moved the question a stage further, and it reappears in exactly the same form. The man or the woman, after all, is only telling and stating, and we are still invited to accept the story upon somebody's authority. The narrator may do his best, and may indeed do so well that to hear his account is as good as having seen what he describes, and nothing could be better than that; the matter might rest there, if this were all. But it must depend considerably on the nature of his story, for it may happen that he tells and describes things that a man is never really in a position to substantiate; his account of himself, for example, cannot be thoroughly valid, not through any want of candour on his part, but simply because no man can completely objectify himself, and a credible account of anything must appear to detach it, to set it altogether free for inspection. And so the novelist passes on towards drama, gets behind the narrator, and represents the mind of the narrator as in itself a kind of action.

By so doing, be it noted, he forfeits none of his special freedom, as I have called it, the picture-making faculty that he enjoys as a story-teller. He is not constrained, like the playwright, to turn his story into dramatic action and nothing else. He has dramatized his novel step by step, until the mind of the picture-maker, Strether or Raskolnikov, is present upon the page; but Strether and Raskolnikov are just as free to project their view of the world, to picture it for the reader, as they might be if they spoke in person. The difference is in the fact that we now see the very sources of the activity within them; we not only share their vision, we watch them absorbing it. Strether in particular, with a mind working so diligently upon every grain of his experience, is a most luminous painter of the world in which he moves—a small circle, but nothing in it escapes him, and he imparts his summary of a thousand matters to the reader; the view that he opens is as panoramic, often enough, as any of Thackeray's sweeping surveys, only the scale is different, with a word barely breathed in place of a dialogue, minutes for months, a turn of a head or an intercepted glance for a chronicle of crime or adulterous intrigue. That liberty, therefore, of standing above the story and taking a broad view of many things, of transcending the limits of the immediate scene —nothing of this is sacrificed by the author's steady advance in the direction of drama. The man's mind has become visible, phenomenal, dramatic; but in acting its part it still lends us eyes, is still an opportunity of extended vision.

It thus becomes clear why the prudent novelist tends to prefer an indirect to a direct method. The simple story-teller begins by addressing himself openly to the reader, and then exchanges this method for another and another, and with each modification he reaches the reader from a further remove. The more circuitous procedure on the part of the author produces a straighter effect for the reader; that is why, other things being equal, the more dramatic way is better than the less. It is indirect, as a method; but it places the thing itself in view, instead of recalling and reflecting and picturing it. For any story, no doubt, there is an ideal point upon this line of progress towards drama, where the author finds the right method of telling the story. The point is indicated by the subject of the story itself, by the particular matter that is to be brought out and made plain; and the author, while he regards the subject and nothing else, is guided to the best manner of treatment by a twofold consideration. In the first place he wishes the story so far as possible to speak for itself, the people and the action to appear independently rather than to be described and explained. To this end the method is raised to the highest dramatic power that the subject allows, until at last, perhaps, it is found that nothing need be explained at all; there need be no revelation of anybody's thought, no going behind any of the appearances on the surface of the action; even the necessary description, as we shall see later on, may be so treated that this too gains the value of drama. Such is the first care of the prudent novelist, and I have dwelt upon it in detail. But it is accompanied and checked by another, not less important.

This is his care for economy; the method is to be pushed as far as the subject can profit by it, but no further. It may happen (for instance in

David Copperfield) that the story *needs* no high dramatic value, and that it would get no advantage from a more dramatic method. If it would gain nothing, it would undoubtedly lose; the subject would be over-treated and would suffer accordingly. Nothing would have been easier than for Dickens to take the next step, as I call it —to treat his story from the point of view of David, but not as David's own narration. Dickens might have laid bare the mind of his hero and showed its operation, as Dostoevsky did with his young man. There was no reason for doing so, however, since the subject is not essentially in David at all, but in the linked fortunes of a number of people grouped around him. David's consciousness, if we watched it instead of listening to his story, would be unsubstantial indeed; Dickens would be driven to enrich it, giving him a more complicated life within; with the result that the centre would be displaced and the subject so far obscured. A story is damaged by too much treatment as by too little, and the severely practical need of true economy in all that concerns a novel is demonstrated once more.

I go no further for the moment, I do not yet consider how the picture of a man's mind is turned into action, induced to assume the look of an objective play. It is a very pretty achievement of art, perhaps the most interesting effect that fiction is able to produce, and I think it may be described more closely. But I return meanwhile to the device of the first person, and to another example of the way in which it is used for its dramatic energy. For my point is so oddly illustrated by the old contrivance of the " epistolary " novel that I cannot omit to glance at it briefly; the kind of enhancement which is sought by the method of The Ambassadors is actually the very same as that which is sought by the method of Clarissa and Grandison. Richardson and Henry James, they are both faced by the same difficulty; one of them is acutely aware of it, and takes very deep-laid precautions to circumvent it; the other, I suppose, does not trouble about the theory of his procedure, but he too adopts a certain artifice which carries him past the particular problem, though at the same time it involves him in several more. Little as Richardson may suspect it, he—and whoever else has the idea of making a story out of a series of letters, or a running diary written from day to day—is engaged in the attempt to show a mind in action, to give a dramatic display of the commotion within a breast. He desires to get into the closest touch with Clarissa's life, and to set the reader in the midst of it; and this is a possible expedient, though it certainly has its drawbacks.

He wishes to avoid throwing Clarissa's agitations into the past and treating them as a historical matter. If they were to become the subject of a record, compiled by her biographer, something would be lost; there would be no longer the same sense of meeting Clarissa afresh, every morning, and of witnessing the new development of her wrongs and woes, already a little more poignant than they were last night. Even if he set Clarissa to write the story in after days, preserving her life for the purpose, she could not quite give us this recurring suspense and shock of sympathy; the lesson of her fortitude would be weakened. Reading her letters, you hear the cry that was wrung from her at the moment; you look forward with her in dismay to the ominous morrow; the spectacle of her bearing under such terrible trials is immediate and urgent. You accompany her step by step, the end still in the future, knowing no more than she how the next corner is to be turned. This is truly to share her life, to lead it by her side, to profit by her example; at any rate her example is eloquently present. Richardson or another, whoever first thought of making her tell her story while she is still in the thick of it, invented a fashion of dramatizing her sensibility that is found to be serviceable occasionally, even now, though scarcely for an enterprise on Clarissa's scale.

Her emotion, like Strether's, is caught in passing; like him she dispenses with the need of a seer, a reflector, some one who will form an impression of her state of mind and reproduce it. The struggles of her heart are not made the material of a chronicle. She reports them, indeed, but at such brief and punctual intervals that her report is like a wheel of life, it reveals her heart in its very pulsation. The queer and perverse idea of keeping her continually bent over her pen—she must have written for many hours every day—has at least this advantage, that for the spectator it keeps her long ordeal always in the foreground. Clarissa's troubles fall within the book, as I have expressed it; they are contemporaneous, they are happening while she writes, this latest agony is a new one since she wrote last, which was only yesterday. Much that is denied to autobiography is thus gained by Clarissa's method, and for her story the advantage is valuable. The subject of her story is not in the distressing events, but in her emotion and her comportment under the strain; how a young gentlewoman suffers and conducts herself in such a situation—that was what Richardson had to show, and the action of the tale is shaped round this question. Lovelace hatches his villainies in order that the subject of the book may be exhaustively illustrated. It is therefore necessary that the conflict within Clarissa should hold the centre, and for this the epistolary method does indeed provide.

Richardson makes the most of it, without doubt; he has strained it to its utmost capacity before he has done with it. A writer who thinks of constructing a novel out of somebody's correspondence may surely consult Clarissa upon all the details of the craft. And Clarissa, and Grandison still more, will also give the fullest warning of the impracticability of the method, after all; for Richardson is forced to pay heavily for its single benefit. He pays with the desperate shifts to which he is driven in order to maintain any kind of verisimilitude. The visible effort of keeping all Clarissa's friends at a distance all the time, so that she may be enabled to communicate only by letter, seems always on the point of bearing him down; while in the case of Grandison it may be said to do so finally, when Miss Byron is reduced to reporting to her friend what another friend has reported concerning Sir Charles's report of his past life among the Italians. I only speak of these wonderful books, however, for the other aspect of their method—because it shows a stage in the natural struggle of the mere record to become something more, to develop independent life and to appear as action. Where the record is one of emotions and senti-ments, delicately traced and disentangled, it is not so easy to see how they may be exposed to an immediate view; and here is a manner, not very handy indeed, but effective in its degree, of meeting the difficulty.

XI

AND now for the method by which the picture of a mind is fully dramatized, the method which is to be seen consistently applied in The Ambassadors and the other later novels of Henry James. How is the author to withdraw, to stand aside, and to let Strether's thought tell its own story? The thing must be seen from our own point of view and no other. Author and hero, Thackeray and Esmond, Meredith and Harry Richmond, have given their various accounts of emotional and intellectual adventure; but they might do more, they might bring the facts of the adventure upon the scene and leave them to make their impression. The story passes in an invisible world, the events take place in the man's mind; and we might have to conclude that they lie beyond our reach, and that we cannot attain to them save by the help of the man himself, or of the author who knows all about him. We might have to make the best of an account at second hand, and it would not occur to us, I dare say, that anything more could be forthcoming; we seem to touch the limit of the possibilities of drama in fiction. But it is not the final limit—there is fiction here

to prove it; and it is this further stroke of the
art that I would now examine.

The world of silent thought is thrown open,
and instead of telling the reader what happened
there, the novelist uses the look and behaviour of
thought as the vehicle by which the story is
rendered. Just as the writer of a play embodies
his subject in visible action and audible speech,
so the novelist, dealing with a situation like
Strether's, represents it by means of the movement that flickers over the surface of his mind.
The impulses and reactions of his mood are the
players upon the new scene. In drama of the
theatre a character must bear his part unaided;
if he is required to be a desperate man, harbour-
ing thoughts of crime, he cannot look to the
author to appear at the side of the stage and
inform the audience of the fact; he must express
it for himself through his words and deeds, his
looks and tones. The playwright so arranges the
matter that these will be enough, the spectator
will make the right inference. But suppose that
instead of a man upon the stage, concealing and
betraying his thought, we watch the thought
itself, the hidden thing, as it twists to and fro in
his brain—watch it without any other aid to
understanding but such as its own manner of
bearing may supply. The novelist, more free
than the playwright, could of course *tell* us, if
he chose, what lurks behind this agitated spirit;
he could step forward and explain the restless
appearance of the man's thought. But if he

prefers the dramatic way, admittedly the more effective, there is nothing to prevent him from taking it. The man's thought, in its turn, can be made to reveal its own inwardness.

Let us see how this plan is pursued in The Ambassadors. That book is entirely concerned with Strether's experience of his peculiar mission to Europe, and never passes outside the circle of his thought. Strether is despatched, it will be remembered, by a resolute New England widow, whose son is living lightly in Paris instead of attending to business at home. To win the hand of the widow, Strether must succeed in snatching the young man from the siren who is believed to have beguiled him. The mission is undertaken in all good faith, Strether descends upon Paris with a mind properly disposed and resolved. He comes as an ambassador representing principle and duty, to treat with the young man, appeal to him convincingly and bear him off. The task before him may be difficult, but his purpose is simple. Strether has reckoned, however, without his imagination; he had scarcely been aware of possessing one before, but everything grows complicated as it is touched and awakened on the new scene. By degrees and degrees he changes his opinion of the life of freedom; it is most unlike his prevision of it, and at last his purpose is actually inverted. He no longer sees a mis-guided young man to be saved from disaster, he sees an exquisite, bountiful world laid at a young man's feet; and now the only question is whether the young man is capable of meeting and grasping his opportunity. He is incapable, as it turns out; when the story ends he is on the verge of rejecting his freedom and going back to the world of commonplace; Strether's mission has ended successfully. But in Strether's mind the revolution is complete; there is nothing left for him, no reward and no future. The world of commonplace is no longer *his* world, and he is too late to seize the other; he is old, he has missed the opportunity of youth.

This is a story which must obviously be told from Strether's point of view, in the first place. The change in his purpose is due to a change in his vision, and the long slow process could not be followed unless his vision were shared by the reader. Strether's predicament, that is to say, could not be placed upon the stage; his outward behaviour, his conduct, his talk, do not express a tithe of it. Only the brain behind his eyes can be aware of the colour of his experience, as it passes through its innumerable gradations; and all understanding of his case depends upon seeing these. The way of the author, therefore, who takes this subject in hand, is clear enough at the outset. It is a purely pictorial subject, covering Strether's field of vision and bounded by its limits; it consists entirely of an impression received by a certain man. There can accordingly be no thought of rendering him as a figure seen from without; nothing that any one else could discern, looking at him and listening to his conversation, would give the full sense of the eventful life he is leading within. The dramatic method, as we ordinarily understand it, is ruled out at once. Neither as an action set before the reader without interpretation from within, nor yet as an action pictured for the reader by some other onlooker in the book, can this story possibly be told.

Strether's real situation, in fact, is not his open and visible situation, between the lady in New England and the young man in Paris; his grand adventure is not expressed in its incidents. These, as they are devised by the author, are secondary, they are the extension of the moral event that takes place in the breast of the ambassador, his change of mind. That is the very middle of the subject; it is a matter that lies solely between Strether himself and his vision of the free world. It is a delightful effect of irony, indeed, that he should have accomplished his errand after all, in spite of himself; but the point of the book is not there, the ironic climax only serves to bring out the point more sharply. The reversal of his own idea is underlined and enhanced by the reversal of the young man's idea in the opposite sense; but essentially the subject of the book would be unchanged if the story ended differently, if the young man held to his freedom and refused to go home. Strether would still have passed through the same cycle of unexpected experience; his errand might have failed, but still it would not have been any the more impossible for him to claim his reward, for his part, than it is impossible as things are, with the quest achieved and the young man ready to hasten back to duty of his own accord. And so the subject can only be reached through Strether's consciousness, it is plain; that way alone will command the impression that the scene makes on him. Nothing in the scene has any importance, any value in itself; what Strether sees in it—that is the whole of its meaning.

But though in The Ambassadors the point of view is primarily Strether's, and though it *appears* to be his throughout the book, there is in fact an insidious shifting of it, so artfully contrived that the reader may arrive at the end without suspecting the trick. The reader, all unawares, is placed in a better position for an understanding of Strether's history, better than the position of Strether himself. Using his eyes, we see what *he* sees, we are possessed of the material on which his patient thought sets to work; and that is so far well enough, and plainly necessary. All the other people in the book face towards him, and it is that aspect of them, and that only, which is shown to the reader; still more important, the beautiful picture of Paris and spring-time, the stir and shimmer of life in the Rue de Rivoli and the gardens of the Tuileries, is Strether's picture, *his* vision, rendered as the time and the place strike upon his senses. All this on which his thought ruminates, the stuff that occupies it, is represented from his point of

161

view. To see it, even for a moment, from some
different angle—if, for example, the author inter-
posed with a vision of his own—would patently
disturb the right impression. The author does no
such thing, it need hardly be said.

When it comes to Strether's treatment of this
material, however, when it is time to learn what
he makes of it, turning his experience over and
over in his mind, then his own point of view no
longer serves. How is anybody, even Strether, to
see the working of his own mind? A mere account
of its working, after the fact, has already been
barred; we have found that this of necessity is
lacking in force, it is statement where we look
for demonstration. And so we must see for
ourselves, the author must so arrange matters
that Strether's thought will all be made intelligible
by a direct view of its surface. The immediate
flaw or ripple of the moment, and the next and
the next, will then take up the tale, like the
speakers in a dialogue which gradually unfolds
the subject of the play. Below the surface,
behind the outer aspect of his mind, we do not
penetrate;   this is drama, and in drama the
spectator must judge by appearances. When
Strether's mind is dramatized, nothing is shown
but the passing images that anybody might
detect, looking down upon a mind grown visible.
There is no drawing upon extraneous sources of
information; Henry James knows all there is to
know of Strether, but he most carefully refrains
from using his knowledge. He wishes us to

THE CRAFT OF FICTION

accept nothing from him, on authority—only to watch and learn.

For suppose him to begin sharing the knowledge that he alone possesses, as the author and inventor of Strether; suppose that instead of representing only the momentary appearance of Strether's thought he begins to expound its substance: he must at once give us the whole of it, must let us into every secret without delay, or his exposition is plainly misleading. It is assumed that he tells all, if he once begins. And so, too, if the book were cast autobiographically and Strether spoke in person; he could not hold back, he could not heighten the story of his thought with that touch of suspense, waiting to be resolved, which stamps the impression so firmly into the memory of the onlooker. In a tale of murder and mystery there is one man who cannot possibly be the narrator, and that is the murderer himself; for if he admits us into his mind at all he must do so without reserve, thereby betraying the secret that we ought to be guessing at for ourselves. But by this method of The Ambassadors the mind of which the reader is made free, Strether's mind, is not given away; there is no need for it to yield up all its secrets at once. The story in it is played out by due degrees, and there may be just as much deliberation, refrainment, suspension, as in a story told scenically upon the stage. All the effect of true drama is thus at the disposal of the author, even when he seems to be describing and

picturing the consciousness of one of his characters. He arrives at the point where apparently
nothing but a summary and a report should be
possible, and even there he is precluded from
none of the privileges of a dramatist.

It is necessary to show that in his attitude
towards his European errand Strether is slowly
turning upon himself and looking in another
direction. To announce the fact, with a tabula-
tion of his reasons, would be the historic, retrospective, undramatic way of dealing with the
matter. To bring his mind into view at the
different moments, one after another, when it is
brushed by new experience—to make a little
scene of it, without breaking into hidden depths
where the change of purpose is proceeding—to
multiply these glimpses until the silent change is
apparent, though no word has actually been said
of it: this is Henry James's way, and though the
method could scarcely be more devious and
roundabout, always refusing the short cut, yet
by these very qualities and precautions it finally
produces the most direct impression, for the
reader has *seen*. That is why the method is
adopted. The author has so fashioned his book
that his own part in the narration is now unobtrusive to the last degree; he, the author,
could not imaginably figure there more discreetly.
His part in the effect is no more than that of the
playwright, who vanishes and leaves his people to
act the story; only instead of men and women
talking together, in Strether's case there are in-

numerable images of thought crowding across the stage, expressing the story in their behaviour.

But there is more in the book, as I suggested just now, than Strether's vision and the play of his mind. In the *scenic* episodes, the colloquies that Strether holds, for example, with his sympathetic friend Maria Gostrey, another turn appears in the author's procedure. Throughout these clear-cut dialogues Strether's point of view still reigns; the only eyes in the matter are still his, there is no sight of the man himself as his companion sees him. Miss Gostrey is clearly visible, and Madame de Vionnet and little Bilham, or whoever it may be; the face of Strether himself is never turned to the reader. On the evening of the first encounter between the elderly ambassador and the young man, they sat together in a café of the boulevards and walked away at midnight through quiet streets; and all through their interview the fact of the young man's appearance is strongly dominant, for it is this that first reveals to Strether how the young man has been transformed by his commerce with the free world; and so his ngure is sharply before the reader as they talk. How Strether seemed to Chad—this, too, is represented, but only by implication, through Chad's speech and manner. It is essential, of course, that it should be so, the one-sided vision is strictly enjoined by the method of the whole book. But though the seeing eye is still with Strether, there is a noticeable change in the author's way with him.

In these scenic dialogues, on the whole, we seem to have edged away from Strether's consciousness. He sees, and we with him; but when he *talks* it is almost as though we were outside him and away from him altogether. Not always, indeed; for in many of the scenes he is busily brooding and thinking throughout, and we share his mind while he joins in the talk. But still, on the whole, the author is inclined to leave Strether alone when the scene is set. He talks the matter out with Maria, he sits and talks with Madame de Vionnet, he strolls along the boulevards with Chad, he lounges on a chair in the Champs Elysées with some one else—we know the kind of scene that is set for Strether, know how very few accessories he requires, and know that the scene marks a certain definite climax, wherever it occurs, for all its everyday look. The occasion is important, there is no doubt about that; its importance is in the air. And Strether takes his part in it as though he had almost become what he cannot be, an objective figure for the reader. Evidently he cannot be that, since the centre of vision is still within him; but by an easy sleight of hand the author gives him almost the value of an independent person, a man to whose words we may listen expectantly, a man whose mind is screened from us. Again and again the stroke is accomplished, and indeed there is nothing mysterious about it. Simply it consists in treating the scene as dramatically as possible—keeping it framed in Strether's vision, certainly, but keeping his consciousness out of sight, his thought un-explored. He talks to Maria; and to us, to the reader, his voice seems as much as hers to belong to somebody whom we are *watching*—which is impossible, because our point of view is his.

A small matter, perhaps, but it is interesting as a sign, still another, of the perpetual tendency of the novel to capture the advantages which it appears to forego. The Ambassadors is without doubt a book that deals with an entirely non-dramatic subject; it is the picture of an *état d'âme*. But just as the chapters that are concerned with Strether's soul are in the key of drama, after the fashion I have described, so too the episode, the occasion, the scene that crowns the impression, is always more dramatic in its method than it apparently has the means to be. Here, for instance, is the central scene of the whole story, the scene in the old Parisian garden, where Strether, finally filled to the brim with the sensation of all the life for which his own oppor-tunity has passed, overflows with his passionate exhortation to little Bilham—warning him, adjur-ing him not to make *his* mistake, not to let life slide away ungrasped. It is the hour in which Strether touches his crisis, and the first necessity of the chapter is to show the sudden lift and heave of his mood within; the voices and admonitions of the hour, that is to say, must be heard and felt as he hears and feels them himself. The scene, then, will be given as Strether's impression, clearly, and so it is; the old garden and the evening light and the shifting company of people appear as their reflection in his thought. But the scene is *also* a piece of drama, it strikes out of the book with the strong relief of dramatic action; which is evidently an advantage gained, seeing the importance of the hour in the story, but which is an advantage that it could not enjoy, one might have said.

The quality of the scene becomes clear if we imagine the story to be told by Strether himself, narrating in the first person. Of the damage that this would entail for the picture of his brooding mind I have spoken already; but suppose the book to have taken the form of autobiography, and suppose that Strether has brought the story up to this point, where he sits beside little Bilham in Gloriani's garden. He describes the deep and agitating effect of the scene upon him, calling to him of the world he has missed; he tells what he thought and felt; and then, he says, I broke out with the following tirade to little Bilham—and we have the energetic outburst which Henry James has put into his mouth. But is it not clear how the incident would be weakened, so rendered? That speech, word for word as we have it, would lose its unexpected and dramatic quality, because Strether, arriving at it by narration, could not suddenly spring away from himself and give the impression of the worn, intelligent, clear-sighted man sitting there in the evening sun, strangely moved to unwonted eloquence. His narration must have discounted the effect of his outburst,

leading us up to the very edge of it, describing
how it arose, explaining where it came from. He
would be *subjective*, and committed to remain so
all the time.

Henry James, by his method, can secure this
effect of drama, even though his Strether is
apparently in the position of a narrator throughout. Strether's are the eyes, I said, and they are
more so than ever during this hour in the garden ;
he is the sentient creature in the scene. But the
author, who all through the story has been
treating Strether's consciousness as a play, as an
action proceeding, can at any moment use his
talk almost as though the source from which it
springs were unknown to us from within.   I
remember that he himself, in his critical preface
to the book, calls attention to the way in which a
conversation between Strether and Maria Gostrey,
near the beginning, puts the reader in possession
of all the past facts of the situation which it is
necessary for him to know ; a *scene* thus takes the
place of that " harking back to make up," as he
calls it, which is apt to appear as a lump of
narrative shortly after the opening of a story.
If Strether were really the narrator, whether in
the first person or the third, he could not use his
own talk in this manner ; he would have to tell
us himself about his past. But he has never *told*
us his thought, we have looked at it and drawn
our inferences ; and so there is still some air of
dramatic detachment about him, and his talk
may seem on occasion to be that of a man whom

we know from outside. The advantage is peculiarly felt on that crucial occasion at Gloriani's, where Strether's sudden flare of vehemence, so natural and yet so unlike him, breaks out with force unimpaired. It strikes freshly on the ear, the speech of a man whose inmost perturbations we have indeed inferred from many glimpses of his mind, but still without ever learning the full tale of them from himself.

The Ambassadors, then, is a story which is seen from one man's point of view, and yet a story in which that point of view is itself a matter for the reader to confront and to watch constructively. Everything in the novel is now dramatically rendered, whether it is a page of dialogue or a page of description, because even in the page of description nobody is addressing us, nobody is reporting his impression to the reader. The impression is enacting itself in the endless series of images that play over the outspread expanse of the man's mind and memory. When the story passes from these to the scenes of dialogue—from the silent drama of Strether's meditation to the spoken drama of the men and women—there is thus no break in the method. The same law rules everywhere—that Strether's changing sense of his situation shall appeal directly to the onlooker, and not by way of any summarizing picture-maker. And yet *as a whole* the book is all pictorial, an indirect impression received through Strether's intervening consciousness, beyond which the story never strays.

I conclude that on this paradox the art of dramatizing the picture of somebody's experience—the art I have been considering in these last chapters —touches its limit. There is indeed no further for it to go.

XII

THERE is no further for it to go, for it now covers the whole story. Henry James was the first writer of fiction, I judge, to use all the possibilities of the method with intention and thoroughness, and the full extent of the opportunity which is thus revealed is very great. The range of method is permanently enlarged; it is proved, once for all, that the craft of fiction has larger resources than might have been suspected before. A novelist in these days is handling an instrument, it may be said, the capacity of which has been very elaborately tested; and though in any particular case there may be good reason why its dramatic effects should not be exhausted— the subject may need none or few of them—yet it must be supposed that the novelist is aware of the faculties that he refuses. There are kinds of virtuosity in any art which affect the whole of its future; painting can never be the same again after some painter has used line and colour in a manner that his predecessors had not fully developed, music makes a new demand of all musicians when one of them has once increased its language. And the language of the novel, extended to the point which it has reached, gives a possible scope to a novelist which he is evidently bound to take into account.

It is a scope so wide and so little explored hitherto that the novel may now be starting upon a fresh life, after the tremendous career it has had already. The discovery of the degree to which it may be enhanced dramatically—this may be a point of departure from which it will set out with vigour renewed; perhaps it has done so by this time. Anyhow it is clear that an immense variety of possible modulations, mixtures, harmonies of method, yet untried, are open to it if it chooses to avail itself; and I should imagine that to a novelist of to-day, entering the field at this late hour, the thought might be a stimulating one. There is still so much to be done, after a couple of centuries of novel-writing without a pause; there are unheard-of experiments to be made. A novel such as The Ambassadors may give no more than a hint of the rich and profound effects waiting to be achieved by the laying of method upon method, and criticism may presently be called on to analyse the delicate process much more closely than I now attempt; it is to be hoped so indeed. Meanwhile it is useful to linger over a book that suggests these possibilities, and to mark the direction in which they seem to point.

The purpose of the novelist's ingenuity is always the same; it is to give to his subject the highest relief by which it is capable of profiting. And the less dramatic, strictly speaking, the subject may be—the less it is able, that is to say, to express itself in action and in action only—the more it is needful to heighten its flat, pictorial, descriptive surface by the arts of drama. It is not managed by peppering the surface with animated dialogue, by making the characters break into talk when they really have nothing to contribute to the subject; the end of this is only to cheapen and discredit their talk when at length it is absolutely required. The dramatic rule is applied more fundamentally; it animates the actual elements of the picture, the description, and makes a drama of these. I have noted how in The Ambassadors the picture of Strether's mind is transformed into an enacted play, even where his story, for chapters at a time, is bare of action in the literal sense. The result, no doubt, is that his mind emerges from the book with force and authority, its presence is _felt._ And now I would track the same method and measure the result in another book, The Wings of the Dove, where the value of this kind of dramatization is perhaps still more clearly to be seen. Again we are dealing with a subject that in the plain meaning of the word is entirely undramatic.

Milly, the Dove, during all that part of the book in which her mind lies open—in the chapters which give her vision of the man and the girl, Densher and Kate, not theirs of her—is hoarding in silence two facts of profoundest import to herself; one is her love for Densher, the other the mortal disease with which she is stricken. It is of these two facts that Kate proposes to take advantage, and there is nothing weak or vague about Kate's design. She and Densher are penniless, Milly is rich, but they can afford to bide their time and Milly cannot; let them do so, therefore, let Densher accept his opportunity, and let him presently return to Kate, well endowed by the generosity of an exquisite young wife, dead in her prime. That is how Milly's condition is to be turned to account by a remarkably clear-headed young woman; but Milly herself is still unaware of any confederation between her two friends, and she silently broods over the struggle in her mind—her desire for life, her knowledge of her precarious hold on life. The chapters I speak of are to give the sense of this conflict, to show unmistakably the pair of facts upon which Kate's project is founded. Milly has nothing to *do* in the story, but she has to *be* with great intensity, for it is on what she is that the story turns. Of that in a moment, however; in these chapters, which are the central chapters of the book, Milly's consciousness is to the fore, the deep agitation within her is the concern of the moment.

Once more it is the superficial play of thought that is put before us. The light stir and vibration of Milly's sensibility from hour to hour is all we actually see; for the most part it is very light, very easy and airy, as she moves with her odd poetry and grace and freedom. She comes from New York, it will be remembered, a " pale angular princess," loaded with millions, and all alone in the world save for her small companion, Mrs. Stringham. She is a rare and innocent creature, receptive and perceptive, thrown into the middle of a situation in which she sees everything, excepting only the scheme by which it is proposed to make use of her. Of that she knows nothing as yet; her troubles are purely her own, and gradually, it is hard to say where or how, we discover what they are. They are much too deeply buried in her mind to appear casually upon the surface at any time; but now and then, in the drama of her meditation, there is a strange look or a pause or a sudden hasty motion which is unexplained, which is portentous, which betrays everything. Presently her great hidden facts have passed into the possession of the reader *whole*, so to speak—not broken into detail, bit by bit, not pieced together descriptively, but so implied and suggested that at some moment or other they spring up complete and solid in the reader's attention. Exactly how and where did it happen? Turning back, looking over the pages again, I can mark the very point, perhaps, at which the thing was liberated and I became possessed of it; I can see the word that finally gave it to me. But at the time it may easily have passed unnoticed; the enlightening word did not seem peculiarly emphatic as it was uttered, it was not announced with any particular circumstance; and yet, presently—there was the piece of knowledge that I had not possessed before.

Not to walk straight up to the fact and put it

into phrases, but to *surround* the fact, and so to detach it inviolate—such is Henry James's manner of dramatizing it. Soon after Milly's first appearance there are some pages that illustrate his procedure very clearly, or very clearly, I should say, when the clue has been picked up and retraced. There is an hour in which Milly gazes open-eyed upon her prospect, measuring its promises and threats, gathering herself for the effort they demand. She sits on a high Italian mountain-ledge, with a blue plain spread out beneath her like the kingdoms of the world; and there she looks at her future with rapt absorption, lost to all other thought. Her mind, if we saw it, would tell us everything then at least; she searches its deepest depth, it is evident. And that is the very reason why her mind should not be exposed in that hour; the troubling shapes that lurk in it are not to be described, they are to make their presence known of their own accord. Instead of intruding upon Milly's lonely rumination, therefore, the author elects to leave her, to join company with her friend in the background, and in that most crucial session to reveal nothing of Milly but the glimpse that her friend catches of her in passing.

The glimpse, so rendered, *tells* nothing. But in Milly's attitude, while she sits enthroned above the world, there is a certain expression, deep and strange, not to be missed, though who shall say exactly what it implies? Is it hope, is it despair? At any rate the clear picture of her remains, and a little later, when her mind is visible again, the memory of her up there on the mountain has quickened the eye of the onlooker. The images in her mind are not at all portentous now; she is among her friends, she is harvesting impressions; there is not a word of anything dark or distressing or ill-omened. But still, but still— we have seen Milly when she believed herself unseen, and it is certain that there is more in her mind than now appears, and though she seems so full of the new excitement of making friends with Kate Croy there must be some preoccupation beneath; and then, in a flash, *these* are the troubles that engage her in solitude, that have ached in her mind, and yet there has never been a single direct allusion to them. Skirting round and round them, giving one brief sight of her in eloquent circumstances, then displaying the all but untroubled surface of her thought on this side and that, the author has encompassed the struggle that is proceeding within her, and has lifted it bodily into the understanding of the reader.

The profit which the story gains from this treatment is easily recognized. Solidity, weight, a third dimension, is given to the impression of Milly's unhappy case. Mere emphasis, a simple underlining of plain words, could never produce the same effect. What is needed is some method which will enable an onlooker to see round the object, to left and right, as far as possible, just as with two eyes, stereoscopically, we shape and solidify the flat impression of a sphere. By such a method the image will be so raised out of its setting that the stream of vision will wash it on either side, leaving no doubt of its substantial form. And so, dealing with the case of Milly, Henry James proceeds to cut behind it, lavishing his care on any but its chief and most memorable aspect. That may wait; meanwhile the momentary flutter of her nerves and fancies is closely noted, wherever her life touches the lives about her, or the few of them that are part of her story. The play draws a steady curve around the subject in the midst; more and more of this outer rim of her consciousness moves into sight. She is seen in the company of the different people who affect her nearly, but in all their intercourse the real burden of her story is veiled under the trembling, wavering delicacy of her immediate thought. Her manner of living and thinking and feeling in the moment is thus revealed in a wide sweep, and at last the process is complete; her case is set free, stands out, and casts its shadow.

These difficulties, these hopes and fears that have been buried in silence, are all included in the sphere of experience which the author has rounded; and by leaving them where they lie he has given us a sense of their substance, of the space they occupy, which we could not have acquired from a straight, square account of them. Milly desired to live, she had every reason in the world for so desiring, and she knew, vaguely at first, then with certainty, that she had no life to hope for; it is a deep agitation which is never at

THE CRAFT OF FICTION

rest. It is far out of sight; but its influence spreads in every direction, and here and there it must touch the surface, even one upon which appearances are maintained so valiantly. And if the surface (which is all we know) is thus high above the depths, and yet there are instants when it is just perceptibly disturbed by things unseen, is it not proved, as it could be proved in no other way, how active and forcible they must be? By no picture of them but by an enactment of their remotest manifestations—that is how their strength, their bulk, their range in a harassed existence is represented. Such is the object gained by the method of dramatization, applied in this way (as with Strether) to the story of a mind. Milly's case, which seemed to be as pictorial, as little dramatic, as could be—since it is all a condition and a situation to be portrayed, not an action—has been turned into drama, the advantages of drama have been annexed on its behalf. There is no action, properly speaking, and yet the story of her troubles has acted itself before our eyes, as we followed the transient expression of her mood.

And now look at a single scene, later on, when the issue of Milly's situation has at last been precipitated. Look, for example, at the scene in which good Susan Stringham, her faithful companion, visits Densher in his Venetian lodging, on an evening of wild autumn rain, to make a last and great appeal to him. An appeal for what? Milly, in her palace hard by, lies stricken, she has

" turned her face to the wall." The vision of hope which had supported her is at an end, not by reason of her mere mortal illness, but because of some other blow which has fallen. Susan knows what it is, and Densher is to learn. Till lately Milly was living in ignorance of the plot woven about her, the masterly design to make use of her in order that Densher and Kate Croy may come together in the end. The design was Kate's from the first; Densher has been much less resolute, but Kate was prepared to see it through. Conceal from Milly that an old engagement holds between her two friends, persuade her that neither has any interest in the other, and all will go well. Milly, believing in Densher's candour, will fall into the plot and enjoy her brief happiness. It cannot be more than brief, for Milly is certainly doomed. But when she dies, and Densher is free for Kate again, who will be the worse for the fraud? Milly will have had what she wants, her two friends will have helped themselves in helping her. So Kate argues plausibly; but it all depends on keeping poor exquisite Milly safely in the dark. If she should discover that Kate and Densher are in league to profit by her, it would be a sharper stroke than the discovery of her malady. And by this autumn evening, when Susan Stringham appears before Densher, Milly *has* discovered—has learned that she has been tricked, has lost her desire of life, has turned her face to the wall.

Susan appears, big with the motive that has

brought her. This visit of hers is an appeal to Densher, so much is clear in all her looks and tones. There is only one way to save Milly, to restore to Milly, not indeed her life, but her desire of it. Densher has it in his power to make her wish to live again, and that is all that he or any one else could achieve for her. The thought is between him and the good woman as they talk; the dialogue, with its allusions and broken phrases, slowly shapes itself to the form of the suppressed appeal. It hangs in the air, almost visibly, before it is uttered at all; and by that time a word is enough, one stroke, and the nature of the appeal and all its implications are in view. The scene has embodied it; the cheerless little room and the falling light and Densher's uneasy movements and Susan's flushed, rain-splashed earnestness have all contributed; the broken phrases, without touching it, have travelled about it and revealed its contour. Densher might tell Milly that she is wrong, might convince her that he and Kate have not beguiled and misled her as she supposes; Densher, in other words, might mislead her again, and Mrs. Stringham entreats him to do so. That is why she has come, and such is the image which has been gradually created, and which at last is actual and palpable in the scene. It has not appeared as a statement or an announcement; Susan's appeal and Densher's tormented response to it are *felt*, establishing their presence as matters which the reader has lived with for the time. They have emerged out of the surface of the scene into form and relief.

And finally the subject of the whole book is rendered in the same way. The subject is not in Milly herself, but in her effect upon the relation existing between Densher and Kate. At the beginning of the book these two are closely allied, and by the end their understanding has been crossed by something that has changed it for ever. Milly has come and gone, nothing is afterwards the same. Their scheme has been successful, for Milly in dying has bequeathed a fortune to Densher. But also she has bequeathed the memory of her last signal to them, which was one that neither could foresee and which the man at any rate could never forget. For Densher had *not* practised that final disloyalty which was begged of him, and Milly had died in full knowledge of their design, and yet she had forgiven. dove-like to the end, and her forgiveness stands between them. Kate recognizes it in the word on which the book closes—" We shall never be again as we were." Whether they accept the situation, whether they try to patch up their old alliance—these questions are no affair of the story. With Kate's word the story is finished; the first fineness of their association is lost, nothing will restore it. Milly has made the change by being what she was, too rare an essence for vulgar uses. Those who wanted the intelligence to understand her must pay their penalty; at least they are intelligent enough to see it.

It is once more the picture of a moral, emotional revolution, the kind of subject that seems to demand a narrator. The story is so little a matter of action that when the revolution is complete there is nothing more to be said. Its result in action is indifferent; the man and the woman may marry or part, the subject is unaffected either way. The progress of the tale lies in the consciousness of the people in it, and somebody is needed, it might have been supposed, to tell us how it all came to pass. Not the author, perhaps, or any of the characters in person; but at least it must be told, at any given juncture, from somebody's point of view, composing and reflecting the story of an experience. But in The Wings of the Dove there is next to no narrative at all, strictly speaking. Who is there that narrates? The author a little, it is true, for the people have to be described, placed, brought on the scene to begin with. But afterwards? Densher, Kate, Milly, Susan Stringham, each in turn *seems* to take up the story and to provide the point of view, and where it is absolutely needful they really do so; they give the mirror for the visible scene about them, Alpine heights, London streets, Venetian palaces. But that is incidental; of the progress of the tale they offer no account. They *act* it, and not only in their spoken words, but also and much more in the silent drama that is perpetually going forward within them. They do not describe and review and recapitulate this drama, nor does the author. It is played before us, we see its actual movement.

The effect is found here and there in all well-made fiction, of course. The undercutting, as I call it, of a flat impression is seen wherever a turn of events is carefully prepared and deliberately approached. But I do not know that anywhere, except in the later novels of Henry James, a pictorial subject is thus handed over in its entirety to the method of drama, so that the intervention of a seeing eye and a recording hand, between the reader and the subject, is practically avoided altogether. I take it as evident that unless the presence of a seer and a recorder is made a value in itself, contributing definitely to the effect of the subject, he is better dispensed with and put out of the way; where other things are equal a direct view of the matter in hand is the best. But it has been made clear in the fore-going pages, I hope, that the uses of a narrator are many and various; other things are *not* equal where the subject asks for no more than to be reflected and pictured. In that case the narrator, standing in front of the story, is in a position to make the most of it, all that can be made; and so he represents the great principle of economy, and is a value in himself, and does contribute to the effect. Many a story, from the large panoramic chronicle to the small and single impression, postulates the story-teller, the picture-maker, and by that method gives its best. Speaking in person or reported obliquely, the narrator serves his turn. But where there is no positive reason for him there is a reason, equally positive, for a different method, one that assigns the point of view to the reader himself. An undramatic subject, we find, can be treated dramatically, so that the different method is at hand.

The story that is concerned, even entirely concerned, with the impact of experience upon a mind (Strether's, say) can be enhanced to the pitch of drama, because thought has its tell-tale gestures and its speaking looks, just as much as an actor on the stage. Make use of these looks and gestures, express the story through them, leave them to enact it—and you have a story which in its manner is effectually drama. Method upon method, the vision *of* a vision, the process of thinking and feeling and seeing exposed objectively to the view of the reader—it is an ingenious art; criticism seems to have paid it less attention than it deserves. But criticism has been hindered, perhaps, by the fact that these books of Henry James's, in which the art is written large, are so odd and so personal and so peculiar in all their aspects. When the whole volume is full of a strongly-marked idiosyncrasy, quite unlike that of anyone else, it is difficult to distinguish between this, which is solely the author's, and his method of treating a story, which is a general question, discussible apart. And thus it happens that the novelist who carried his research into the theory of the art further than any other—the only real *scholar* in the art—is the novelist whose methods are most likely to be overlooked or mistaken, regarded as simply a part of his own original quiddity. It should be possible to isolate them, to separate them in thought from the temperament by which they were coloured; they belong to the craft, which belongs to no man in particular. They still wait to be fully assimilated into the criticism of fiction; there is much more in them, no doubt, than the few points that I touch on here. But I pass on to one or two of the rest.

XIII

WHAT, then, is a dramatic subject? Hitherto I have been speaking of novels in which some point of view, other than that of the reader, the impartial onlooker, is prescribed by the subject in hand. In big chronicles like Thackeray's it is clear that the controlling point of view can only be that of the chronicler himself, or of some one whom he sets up to tell the story on his behalf. The expanse of life which the story covers is far too great to be shown to the reader in a series of purely dramatic scenes. It is absolutely necessary for the author or his spokesman to draw back for a general view of the matter from time to time; and whenever he does so the story becomes *his* impression, summarized and pictured for the reader. In Esmond or The Virginians or The Newcomes, there are tracts and tracts of the story which are bound to remain outside the reader's direct vision; only a limited number of scenes and occasions could possibly be set forth in the form of drama. A large, loose, manifold subject, in short, extensive in time and space, full of crowds and diversions, is a pictorial subject and can be nothing else. However intensely it may be dramatized here and there, on the whole it must be presented as a conspectus,

the angle of vision being assigned to the narrator.
It is simply a question of amount, of quantity,
of the reach of the subject. If it passes a certain
point it exceeds the capacity of the straight and
dramatic method.

Madame Bovary and The Ambassadors, again,
are undramatic in their matter, though their
reach is comparatively small; for in both of
them the emphasis falls upon changes of mind,
heart, character, gradually drawn out, not upon
any clash or opposition resolved in action. They
might be treated scenically, no doubt; their
authors might conceivably have handled them
in terms of pure drama, without any direct display of Emma's secret fancies or Strether's
brooding imagination. But in neither case could
that method make the most of the subject or
bring out all that it has to give. The most
expressive, most enlightening part of Strether's
story lies in the reverberating theatre of his mind,
and as for Emma, the small exterior facts of her
story are of very slight account. Both these books,
therefore, in their general lines, are pictured impressions, not actions—even though in Bovary
to some extent, and in The Ambassadors almost
wholly, the picture is itself dramatized in the
fashion I have indicated. That last effect belongs only to the final method, the treatment
of the surface; underneath it there is in both the
projection of a certain person's point of view.

But now look at the contrast in The Awkward
Age, a novel in which Henry James followed a

single method throughout, from top to bottom, denying himself the help of any other. He chose to treat this story as pure drama ; he never once draws upon the characteristic resource of the novelist—who is able, as the dramatist is not able, to give a generalized and foreshortened account of the matter in hand. In The Awkward Age everything is immediate and particular ; there is no insight into anybody's thought, no survey of the scene from a height, no resumption of the past in retrospect. The whole of the book passes scenically before the reader, and nothing is offered but the look and the speech of the charac-ters on a series of chosen occasions. It might indeed be printed as a play ; whatever is not dialogue is simply a kind of amplified stage-direction, adding to the dialogue the expressive effect which might be given it by good acting. The novelist, using this method, claims only one advantage over the playwright ; it is the advan-tage of ensuring the very best acting imaginable, a performance in which every actor is a perfect artist and not the least point is ever missed. The play is not handed over to the chances of interpretation—that is the difference ; the author creates the manner in which the words are spoken, as well as the words themselves, and he may keep the manner at an ideal pitch. Otherwise the novelist completely ties his hands, submitting to all the restraints of the playwright in order to secure the compactness and the direct force of true drama.

THE CRAFT OF FICTION

What is the issue of a certain conjunction of circumstances? The subject of the book is in the question. First of all we see a highly sophisticated circle of men and women, who seem so well practised in the art of living that they could never be taken by surprise. Life in their hands has been refined to a process in which nothing appears to have been left to chance. Their intelligence accounts for everything; they know where they are, they know what they want, and under a network of discretion which they all sustain they thoroughly understand each other. It is a charmed world, altogether self-contained, occupying a corner of modern London. It is carefully protected within and without; and yet oddly enough there is one quite common and regular contingency for which it is not prepared at all. Its handling of life proceeds smoothly so long as all the men and women together are on a level of proficiency, all alike experienced in the art; and they can guard themselves against intruders from elsewhere. But periodically it must happen that their young grow up; the daughter of the house reaches the " awkward age," becomes suddenly too old for the school-room and joins her elders below. Then comes the difficulty; there is an interval in which she is still too young for the freedom of her elders' style, and it looks as though she might disconcert them not a little, sitting there with wide eyes. Do they simply disregard her and continue their game as before? Do they try to adapt their style

to her inexperience? Apparently they have no
theory of their proper course; the difficulty
seems to strike them afresh, every time that it
recurs. In other such worlds, not of modern
London, it is foreseen and provided for; the
young woman is married and launched at once,
there is no awkward age. But here and now—or
rather here and *then*, in the nineteenth century—
it makes a real little situation, and this is the
subject of Henry James's book.

It is clearly dramatic; it is a clean-cut situation, raising the question of its issue, and by
answering the question the subject is treated.
What will these people do, how will they circumvent this awkwardness? That is what the book
is to show—action essentially, not the picture of
a character or a state of mind. Mind and character enter into it, of course, as soon as the situation
is particularized; the girl becomes an individual,
with her own outlook, her own way of reaching
a conclusion, and her point of view must then
be understood. But whatever it may be, it does
not constitute the situation. That is there in
advance, it exists in general, and the girl comes
upon the scene, like the rest of the people in the
book, to illustrate it. The subject of the book
lies in their behaviour; there are no gradual
processes of change and development to be
watched in their minds, it is their action that is
significant. By clever management the author
can avoid the necessity of looking inside their
motives; these are betrayed by visible and

audible signs. The story proceeds in the open, point by point; from one scene to another it shows its curve and resolves the situation. And very ironic and pleasing and unexpected the resolution proves. It takes everybody by surprise; no one notices what is happening till it is over, but it begins to happen from the start. The girl Nanda, supposably a helpless spectator, takes control of the situation and works it out for her elders. She is the intelligent and expert and self-possessed one of them all; they have only to leave everything to her light manipulation, and the awkwardness—which is theirs, not hers—is surmounted. By the time she has displayed all her art the story is at an end; her action has answered the question and provided the issue.

The theme of the book being what it is, an action merely, and an action strictly limited in its scope, it requires no narrator. In a dozen scenes or so the characters may set it forth on their own account, and we have only to look on; nobody need stand by and expound. The situation involves no more than a small company of people, and there is no reason for them to straggle far, in space or time; on the contrary, the compactness of the situation is one of its special marks. Its point is that it belongs to a little organized circle, a well-defined incident in their lives. And since the root of the matter is in their behaviour, in the manner in which they meet or fail to meet the incident, their behaviour will sufficiently express what is in their minds; it is not as though the theme of the story lay in some slow revulsion or displacement of mood, which it would be necessary to understand before its issue in action could be appreciated. What do they *do*? —that is the immediate question; what they think and feel is a matter that is entirely implied in the answer. Obviously that was not at all the case with Strether. The workings of his imagination spread over far more ground, ramified infinitely further than anything that he *did*; his action depended upon his view of things and logically flowed from it, but his action by itself would give no measure at all of his inner life. With the people of The Awkward Age, on the other hand, their action fully covers their motives and sentiments—or can be made to do so, by the care of a dexterous author.

And so the story can be rendered with absolute consistency, on one method only, if the author chooses. And he does so choose, and The Awkward Age rounds off the argument I have sought to unwind—the sequence of method and method, each one in turn pushing its way towards a completer dramatization of the story. Here at any rate is one book in which a subject capable of acting itself out from beginning to end is made to do so, one novel in which method becomes as consistent and homogeneous as it ever may in fiction. No other manner of telling a story can be quite so true to itself. For whereas drama, in this book, depends not at all upon the author's

" word of honour," and deals entirely with immediate facts, the most undramatic piece of fiction can hardly for long be consistent in its own line, but must seek the support of scenic presentation. Has anyone tried to write a novel in which there should be no dialogue, no immediate scene, nothing at all but a diffused and purely subjective impression? Such a novel, if it existed, would be a counterpart to The Awkward Age. Just as Henry James's book never deviates from the straight, square view of the passing event, so the other would be exclusively oblique, general, retrospective, a meditation upon the past, bringing nothing into the foreground, dramatizing nothing in talk or action.

The visionary fiction of Walter Pater keeps as nearly to a method of that kind, I suppose, as fiction could. In Marius probably, if it is to be called a novel, the art of drama is renounced as thoroughly as it has ever occurred to a novelist to dispense with it. I scarcely think that Marius ever speaks or is spoken to audibly in the whole course of the book; such at least is the impression that it leaves. The scenes of the story reach the reader by refraction, as it were, through the medium of Pater's harmonious murmur. But scenes they must be; not even Pater at his dreamiest can tell a story without incident particularized and caught in the act. When Marius takes a journey, visits a philosopher or enters a church, the event stands out of the past and makes an appeal to the eye, is presented as it takes place; and this is a movement in the direction of drama, even if it goes no further. Pater, musing over the life of his hero, all but lost in the general sentiment of its grace and virtue, is arrested by the definite images of certain hours and occasions; the flow of his rumination is interrupted while he pauses upon these, to make them visible; they must be given a kind of objectivity, some slight relief against the dim background. No story-teller, in short, can use a manner as strictly subjective, as purely personal, as the manner of The Awkward Age is the reverse.

But as for this book, it not only ends one argument, it is also a turning-point that begins another. For when we have seen how fiction gradually aspires to the weight and authority of the thing acted, purposely limiting its own discursive freedom, it remains to see how it resumes its freedom when there is good cause for doing so. It is not for nothing that The Awkward Age is as lonely as it seems to be in its kind. I have seized upon it as an example of the dramatic method pursued *à outrance*, and it is very convenient for criticism that it happens to be there; the book points a sound moral with clear effect. But when it is time to suggest that even in dealing with a subject entirely dramatic, a novelist may well find reason to keep to his old familiar mixed method—*circumspice*: it would appear that he does so invariably. Where are the other Awkward Ages, the many that we might expect if the value of drama is so great? I dare say one might discover a number of small things, short dramatic pieces (I have mentioned the case of Maupassant), which would satisfy the requirement; but on the scale of Henry James's book I know of nothing else. Plenty of people find their theme in matters of action, matters of incident, like the story of Nanda; it is strange that they should not sometimes choose to treat it with strict consistency. How is one to assert a principle which is apparently supported by only one book in a thousand thousand?

I think it must be concluded, in the first place, that to treat a subject with the rigour of Henry James is extremely difficult, and that the practice of the thousand thousand is partly to be explained by this fact. Perhaps many of them would be more dramatically inclined if the way were easier. It must always be simpler for a story-teller to use his omniscience, to dive into the minds of his people for an explanation of their acts, than to make them so act that no such explanation is ever needed. Or perhaps the state of criticism may be to blame, with its long indifference to these questions of theory; or perhaps (to say all) there is no very lively interest in them even among novelists. Anyhow we may say from experience that a novel is more likely to fall below its proper dramatic pitch than to strain beyond it; in most of the books around us there is an easy-going reliance on a narrator of some kind, a showman who is behind the scenes of the story and can tell us all about it. He seems to come forward in many a case without doing the story any particular service; sometimes he actually embarrasses it, when a matter of vivid drama is violently forced into the form of a narration. One can only suspect that he then exists for the convenience of the author. It *is* helpful to be able to say what you like about the characters and their doings in the book; it may be very troublesome to make their doings as expressive as they might be, eloquent enough to need no comment.

Yet to see the issue slowly unfolding and flowering out of the middle of a situation, and to watch it emerge unaided, with everything that it has to say said by the very lines and masses of its structure—this is surely an experience apart, for a novel-reader, with its completeness and cleanness and its hard, pure edge. It is always memorable, it fills the mind so acceptably that a story-teller might be ready and eager to aspire to this effect, one would think, whenever his matter gives him the chance. Again and again I have wished to silence the voice of the spokesman who is supposed to be helping me to a right appreciation of the matter in hand—the author (or his creature) who knows so much, and who pours out his information over the subject, and who talks and talks about an issue that might be revealing itself without him. The spokesman has his way too often, it can hardly be doubted; the instant authority of drama is neglected. It is the day of the deep-breathed narrator, striding from volume to volume as tirelessly as the Scudéries and Calprenèdes of old ; and it is true, no doubt, that the novel (in all languages, too, it would seem) is more than ever inclined to the big pictorial subject, which requires the voluble chronicler ; but still it must happen occasionally that a novelist prefers a dramatic motive, and might cast it into a round, sound action and leave it in that form if he chose. Here again there is plenty of room for enterprise and experiment in fiction, even now.

But at the same time it must be admitted that there is more in the general unwillingness of story-tellers to entrust the story to the people in it—there is more than I have said. If they are much less dramatic than they might be, still it is not to be asserted that a subject will often find perfect expression through the uncompromising method of The Awkward Age. That book itself perhaps suggests, if it does no more than suggest, that drama cannot always do everything in a novel, even where the heart of the story seems to lie in its action. The story of Nanda drops neatly into scenic form—that is obvious ; it is well adapted for treatment as a row of detached episodes or occasions, through which the subject is slowly developed. But it is a question whether a story which requires and postulates such a very particular background, so singular and so artificial, is reasonably denied the licence to make its background as effective as possible, by what-

ever means. Nanda's world is not the kind of
society that can be taken for granted; it is not
modernity in general, it is a small and very
definite tract. For the purposes of her story it is
important that her setting should be clearly seen
and known, and the method of telling her story
must evidently take this into account. Nanda
and her case are not rendered if the quality of the
civilization round her is left in any way doubtful,
and it happens to be a very odd quality indeed.

Henry James decided, I suppose, that it was
sufficiently implied in the action of his book and
needed nothing more; Nanda's little world
would be descried behind the scene without any
further picturing. He may have been right, so
far as The Awkward Age is concerned; the
behaviour of the people in the story is certainly
packed with many meanings, and perhaps it is
vivid enough to enact the general character of
their lives and ways, as well as their situation in
the foreground; perhaps the charmed circle of
Mrs. Brookenham and her wonderful crew is
given all the effect that is needed. But the
question brings me to a clear limitation of drama
on the whole, and that is why I raise it. Here is
a difficulty to which the dramatic method, in its
full severity; is not specially accommodated, one
that is not in the line of its strength. To many of
the difficulties of fiction, as we have seen, it
brings precisely the right instrument; it gives
validity, gives direct force to a story, and to do
so is its particular property. For placing and

establishing a piece of action it is paramount. But where it is not only a matter of placing the action in view, but of relating it to its surroundings, strict drama is at once at a disadvantage. The seeing eye of the author, which can sweep broadly and generalize the sense of what it sees, will meet this difficulty more naturally. Drama reinforcing and intensifying picture we have already seen again and again; and now the process is reversed. From the point of view of the reader, the spectator of the show, the dramatic scene is vivid and compact; but it is narrow, it can have no great depth, and the colour of the atmosphere can hardly tell within the space. It is likely, therefore, that unless this close direct vision is supplemented by a wider survey, fronting the story from a more distant point of view, the background of the action, the manner of life from which it springs, will fail to make its full impression.

It amounts to this, that the play-form—and with it fiction that is purely dramatic in its method—is hampered in its power to express the outlying associations of its scene. It *can* express them, of course; in clever hands it may seem to do so as thoroughly as any descriptive narration. But necessarily it does so with far more expense of effort than the picture-making faculty which lies in the hand of the novelist; and that is in general a good reason why the prudent novelist, with all his tendency to shed his privileges, still clings to this one. It is possible to imagine that a novel might be as bare of all background as a play of Racine; there might be a story in which any hint of continuous life, proceeding behind the action, would simply confuse and distort the right effect. One thinks of the story of the Princesse de Clèves, floating serenely in the void, without a sign of any visible support from a furnished world; and there, no doubt, nothing would be gained by bringing the lucid action to ground and fixing it in its setting. It is a drama of sentiment, needing only to be embodied in characters as far as possible detached from any pictured surroundings, with nothing but the tradition of fine manners that is inherent in their grand names. But wherever the effect of the action depends upon its time and place, a novelist naturally turns to the obvious method if there is no clear reason for refusing it. In The Awkward Age, to look back at it once more, it may be that there is such a reason; the beauty of its resolute consistency is of course a value in itself, and it may be great enough to justify a *tour de force*. But a *tour de force* it is, when a novelist seeks to render the general life of his story in the particular action, and in the action alone; for his power to support the drama pictorially is always there, if he likes to make use of it.

XIV

SINCE he practically always does so, readily enough, it may seem unnecessary to insist upon the matter. Not often have we seen a novelist pushing his self-denial beyond reason, rejecting the easy way for the difficult without good cause. But in order to make sure of breaking a sound rule at the right point, and not before—to take advantage of laxity when strictness becomes unrewarding, and only then—it is as well to work both ways, from the easy extreme to the difficult and back again. The difficult extreme, in fiction, is the dramatic rule absolute and unmitigated; having reached it from the other end, having begun with the pictorial summary and proceeded from thence to drama, we face the same stages reversed. And it is now, I think, that we best appreciate the liberties taken with the resources of the novelist by Balzac. His is a case that should be approached indirectly. If one plunges straight into Balzac, at the beginning of criticism, it is hard to find the right line through the abundance of good and bad in his books; there is so much of it, and all so strong and staring. It looks at first sight as though his good and his bad alike were entirely conspicuous and unmistakable. His devouring passion for life, his

203

grotesque romance, his truth and his falsity, these cover the whole space of the Comédie between them, and nobody could fail to recognize the full force of either. He is tremendous, his taste is abominable—what more is there to say of Balzac? And that much has been said so often, in varied words, that there can be no need to say it again for the ten-thousandth time.

Such is the aspect that Balzac presents, I could feel, when a critic tries to face him immediately; his obviousness seems to hide everything else. But if one passes him by, following the track of the novelist's art elsewhere, and then returns to him with certain definite conclusions, his aspect is remarkable in quite a new way. His badness is perhaps as obvious as before; there is nothing fresh to discover about that. His greatness, however, wears a different look; it is no longer the plain and open surface that it was. It has depths and recesses that did not appear till now, enticing to criticism, promising plentiful illustration of the ideas that have been gathered by the way. One after another, the rarer, obscurer effects of fiction are all found in Balzac, behind his blatant front. He illustrates everything, and the only difficulty is to know where to begin.

The effect of the generalized picture, for example, supporting the play of action, is one in which Balzac particularly delights. He constantly uses it, he makes it serve his purpose with a very high hand. It becomes more than a support, it becomes a kind of propulsive force applied to

the action at the start. Its value is seen
at its greatest in such books as Le Curé de
Village, Père Goriot, La Recherche de l'Absolu,
Eugénie Grandet—most of all, perhaps, in this
last. Wherever, indeed, his subject requires to be
lodged securely in its surroundings, wherever the
background is a main condition of the story,
Balzac is in no hurry to precipitate the action;
that can always wait, while he allows himself the
leisure he needs for massing the force which is
presently to drive the drama on its way. Nobody
gives such attention as Balzac does in many of
his books, and on the whole in his best, to the
setting of the scene; he clearly considers these
preparatory pictures quite as important as the
events which they are to enclose.

And so, in Père Goriot, all the potent life of
the Maison Vauquer is deliberately collected and
hoarded up to the point where it is enough, when
it is let loose, to carry the story forward with a
strong sweep. By the time the story itself is
reached the Maison Vauquer is a fully created
impression, prepared to the last stroke for the
drama to come. Anything that may take place
there will have the whole benefit of its setting,
without more ado; all the rank reality of the
house and its inmates is immediately bestowed
on the action. When the tale of Goriot comes to
the front it is already more than the tale of a
certain old man and his woes. Goriot, on the
spot, is one of Maman Vauquer's boarders, and
the mere fact is enough, by now, to differentiate

him, to single him out among miserable old men. Whatever he does he carries with him the daily experience of the dingy house and the clattering meals and the frowzy company, with Maman Vauquer, hard and hungry and harassed—Mrs. Todgers would have met her sympathetically, they would have understood each other—at the head of it. Into Goriot's yearnings over his fashionable daughters the sounds and sights and smells of his horrible home have all been gathered; they deepen and strengthen his poor story throughout. Balzac's care in creating the scene, therefore, is truly economical; it is not merely a manner of setting the stage for the drama, it is a provision of character and energy for the drama when it begins.

His pictures of country towns, too, Saumur, Limoges, Angoulême, have the same kind of part to play in the Scènes de la vie de province. When Balzac takes in hand the description of a town or a house or a workshop, he may always be suspected, at first, of abandoning himself entirely to his simple, disinterested craving for facts. There are times when it seems that his inexhaustible knowledge of facts is carrying him where it will, till his only conscious purpose is to set down on paper everything that he knows. He is possessed by the lust of description for its own sake, an insatiable desire to put every detail in its place, whether it is needed or no. So it seems, and so it is occasionally, no doubt; there is nothing more tiresome in Balzac than his zest, his delight,

THE CRAFT OF FICTION

his triumph, when he has apparently succeeded in forgetting altogether that he is a novelist. He takes a proper pride in Grandet or Goriot or Lucien, of course; but his heart never leaps quite so high, it might be thought, as when he sees a chance for a discourse upon money or commerce or Italian art. And yet the result is always the same in the end; when he has finished his lengthy research among the furniture of the lives that are to be evoked, he has created a scene in which action will move as rapidly as he chooses, without losing any of its due emphasis. He has illustrated, in short, the way in which a pictorial impression, wrought to the right pitch, will speed the work of drama—will become an effective agent in the book, instead of remaining the mere decorative introduction that it may seem to be.

Thus it is that Balzac was able to pack into a short book—he never wrote a long one—such an effect of crowds and events, above all such an effect of time. Nobody knows how to compress so much experience into two or three hundred pages as Balzac did unfailingly. I cannot think that this is due in the least to the laborious inter-weaving of his books into a single scheme; I could believe that in general a book of Balzac's suffers, rather than gains, by the recurrence of the old names that he has used already elsewhere. It is an amusing trick, but exactly what is its object? I do not speak of the ordinary " sequel," where the fortunes of somebody are followed for another stage, and where the second part is

207

THE CRAFT OF FICTION

simply the continuation of the first in a direct
line. But what of the famous idea of making
book after book overlap and encroach and
entangle itself with the rest, by the device of
setting the hero of one story to figure more or less
obscurely in a dozen others? The theory is, I
suppose, that the characters in the background
and at the corners of the action, if they are
Rastignac and Camusot and Nucingen, retain the
life they have acquired elsewhere, and thereby
swell the life of the story in which they reappear.
We are occupied for the moment with some one
else, and we discover among his acquaintances a
number of people whom we already know; that
fact, it is implied, will add weight and authority
to the story of the man in the foreground—who
is himself, very likely, a man we have met
casually in another book. It ought to make, it
must make, his situation peculiarly real and
intelligible that we find him surrounded by
familiar friends of our own; and that is the
artistic reason of the amazing ingenuity with
which Balzac keeps them all in play.

Less artistic and more mechanical, I take it,
his ingenuity seems than it did of old. I forget
how few are the mistakes and contradictions of
which Balzac has been convicted, in the shuffling
and re-shuffling of his characters; but when his
accuracy has been proved there still remains the
question of its bearing upon his art. I only touch
upon the question from a single point of view,
when I consider whether the density of life in so

many of his short pieces can really owe anything
to the perpetual flitting of the men and women
from book to book. Suppose that for the moment
Balzac is evoking the figure and fortunes of
Lucien de Rubempré, and that a woman who
appears incidentally in his story turns out to be
our well-remembered Delphine, Goriot's daughter.
We know a great deal about the past of Delphine,
as it happens; but at this present juncture, in
Lucien's story, her past is entirely irrelevant. It
belongs to another adventure, where it mattered
exceedingly, an adventure that took place before
Lucien was heard of at all. As for his story, and
for the reality with which it may be endowed,
this depends solely upon our understanding of
his world, *his* experience; and if Delphine's old
affairs are no part of it, our previous knowledge of
her cannot help us with Lucien. It detracts,
rather, from the force of his effect; it sets up a
relation that has nothing to do with him, a
relation between Delphine and the reader, which
only obstructs our view of the world as Lucien
sees it. Of the characters in the remoter planes
of the action (and that is Delphine's position is
his story) no more is expected than their value
for the purpose of the action in the foreground.
That is all that can be *used* in the book; whatever
more they may bring will lie idle, will contribute
nothing, and may even become an embarrassment. The numberless people in the Comédie who
carry their lengthening train of old associations
from book to book may give the Comédie, as a

whole, the look of unity that Balzac desired; that is another point. But in any single story, such of these people as appear by the way, incidentally, must for the time being shed their irrelevant life; if they fail to do so, they disturb the unity of the story and confuse its truth.

Balzac's unrivalled power of placing a figure in its surroundings is not to be explained, then, by his skill in working his separate pieces together into one great web; the design of the Human Comedy, so largely artificial, forced upon it as his purpose widened, is no enhancement of the best of his books. The fullness of experience which is rendered in these is exactly the same—is more expressive, if anything—when they are taken out of their context; it is all to be attributed to their own art. I come back, therefore, to the way in which Balzac handled his vast store of facts, when he set out to tell a story, and made them count in the action which he brought to the fore. He seldom, I think, regards them as material to be disguised, to be given by implication in the drama itself. He is quite content to offer his own impression of the general landscape of the story, a leisurely display which brings us finally to the point of action. Then the action starts forward with a reserve of vigour that helps it in various ways. The more important of these, as I see them, will be dealt with in the next chapter; but meanwhile I may pick out another, one that is often to be seen in Balzac's work and that he needed only too often. It was not the best of his work that needed it ; but the effect I mean is an interesting one in itself, and it appeals to a critic where it occurs. It shows how a novelist, while in general seeking to raise the power of his picture by means of drama, will sometimes reverse the process, deliberately, in order to rescue the power of his drama from becoming violence. If fiction always aims at the appearance of truth, there are times when the dramatic method is too much for it, too searching and too betraying. It leaves the story to speak for itself, but perhaps the story may then say too much to be reasonably credible. It must be restrained, qualified, toned down, in order to make its best effect. Where the action, in short, is likely to seem harsh, overcharged, romantic, it is made to look less so, less hazardous and more real, by recourse to the art of the picture-maker.

Balzac, it cannot be denied, had frequent cause to look about him for whatever means there might be of extenuating, and so of confirming, an incredible story. His passion for truth was often in conflict with his lust for marvels, and the manner in which they were mixed is the chief interest, I dare say, of some of his books. See him, for example, in the Splendeurs et Misères des Courtisanes, trying with one hand to write a novel of Parisian manners, with the other a romance of mystery, and to do full justice to both. Trompe-la-Mort, the Napoleon of crime, and Esther, the inspired courtesan, represent the romance, and Balzac sets himself to absorb the

extravagant tale into a study of actual life. If
he can get the tale firmly embedded in a background of truth, its falsity may be disguised, the
whole book may even pass for a scene of the
human comedy; it may be accepted as a piece of
reality, on the same level, say, as Eugénie Grandet
or Les Parents Pauvres. That is evidently his
aim, and if only his romance were a little less
gaudy, or his truth not quite so true, he would
have no difficulty in attaining it; the action
would be subdued and kept in its place by the
pictorial setting. The trouble is that Balzac's
idea of a satisfying crime is as wild as his hold
upon facts is sober, so that an impossible strain
is thrown upon his method of reconciling the two.
Do what he will, his romance remains staringly
false in its contrast with his reality; there is an
open gap between the wonderful pictures of the
town in Illusions Perdues and the theatrical
drama of the old convict which they introduce.
Yet his method was a right one, though it was
perverse of Balzac to be occupied at all with
such devices, when he might have rejected his
falsity altogether. In another man's work,
where there is never this sharp distinction between true and false, where both are merged into
something different from either—in Dickens's
work—the method I refer to is much more
successfully followed; and there, in any of
Dickens's later books, we find the clearest example
of it.

I have already been reminded of Stevenson's

word upon this matter; Stevenson noted how Dickens's way of dealing with his romantic intrigues was to lead gradually into them, through well-populated scenes of character and humour; so that his world is actual, its air familiar, by the time that his plot begins to thicken. He gives himself an ample margin in which to make the impression of the kind of truth he needs, before beginning to concentrate upon the fabulous action of the climax. Bleak House is a very good case; the highly coloured climax in that book is approached with great skill and caution, all in his most masterly style. A broad stream of diversified life moves slowly in a certain direction, so deliberately at first that its scope, its spread, is much more evident than its movement. The book is a big survey of a quantity of odd and amusing people, and it is only by degrees that the discursive method is abandoned and the narrative brought to a point. Presently we are in the thick of the story, hurrying to the catastrophe, without having noticed at all, it may be, that our novel of manners has turned into a romantic drama, with a mysterious crime to crown it. Dickens manages it far more artfully than Balzac, because his imagination is not, like Balzac's, divided against itself. The world which he peopled with Skimpole and Guppy and the Bayham Badgers was a world that could easily include Lady Dedlock, for though she is perhaps of the theatre, they are certainly not of the common earth. They and she alike are at the same angle to literal fact, they diverging one way, she another; they accordingly make a kind of reality which can assimilate her romance. Dickens was saved from trying to write two books at once by the fact that one completely satisfied him. It expressed the exciting, amazing, exhilarating world he lived in himself, with its consistent transmutation of all values, and he knew no other.

The method which he finally worked out for himself was exactly what he required. There might be much to say of it, for it is by no means simple, but I am only concerned with one or two points in it. The chief characteristic I take to be this careful introduction of violent drama into a scene already prepared to vouch for it—a scene so alive that it compels belief, so queer that almost anything might happen there naturally. The effect which Dickens gets from the picture in his novels, as opposed to the action, is used as a sort of attestation of the action; and it surely fulfils its mission very strikingly in the best of his work—the best from this point of view—Bleak House, Dombey and Son, Our Mutual Friend. His incurable love of labyrinthine mystification, when it really ran away with him, certainly defeated all precautions; not even old Dorrit's Marshalsea, not even Flora and Mr. F.'s Aunt, can do anything to carry off the story of the Clennams. But so long as he was content with a fairly straightforward romance, all went well; the magnificent life that he projected was prepared to receive and to speed it. Blimber and Mrs. Pipchin and Miss Tox, the Podsnaps and Twemlow and the Veneerings, all contribute out of their overflow of energy to the force of a drama —a drama in which they may take no specific part, but which depends on them for the furnishing of an appropriate scene, a favouring background, a world attuned. This and so much more they do that it may seem like insulting them even to think for a moment of their subordination to the general design, which is indeed a great deal less interesting than they. But Dickens's method is sound and good, and not the less so because he used it for comparatively trivial purposes. It is strange that he should have known how to invent such a scene, and then have found no better drama to enact on it—strange and always stranger, with every re-reading. That does not affect his handling of a subject, which is all that I deal with here.

The life which he creates and distributes right and left, in such a book as Bleak House, before bending to his story—this I call his picture, for picture it is in effect, not dramatic action. It exhibits the world in which Lady Dedlock is to meditate murder, the fog of the suit in Chancery out of which the intrigue of the book is to emerge. It is the summary of a situation, with its elements spreading widely and touching many lives; it gathers them in and gives an impression of them all. It is pictorial as a whole, and quite as much so as any of Thackeray's broad visions. But I have noted before how inevitably Dickens's picture, unlike Thackeray's, is presented in the *form* of scenic action, and here is a case in point. All this impression of life, stretching from the fog-bound law courts to the marshes of Chesney Wold, from Krook and Miss Flite to Sir Leicester and Volumnia, is rendered as incident, as a succession of particular occasions—never, or very seldom, as general and far-seeing narrative, after Thackeray's manner. Dickens continually holds to the immediate scene, even when his object is undramatic; he is always readier to work in action and dialogue than to describe at large; he is happier in placing a character there before us, as the man or woman talked and behaved in a certain hour, on a certain spot, than in reflecting a long impression of their manner of living. In Thackeray's hands the life of Miss Flite, for instance, would have become a legend, recalled and lingered over, illustrated by passing glimpses of her ways and oddities. With Dickens she is always a little human being who figures upon a scene, in a group, a visible creature acting her small part; she is always dramatic.

And Dickens, using this method everywhere, even in such a case as hers—even where his purpose, that is to say, is pictorial, to give the sense of a various and vivacious background—is forced to crystallize and formulate his characters very sharply, if they are to make their effect; it is why he is so often reduced to the expedient of labelling his people with a trick or a phrase, which they have to bring with them every time they appear. Their opportunities are strictly limited; the author does not help them out by glancing freely into their lives and sketching them broadly. Flite, Snagsby, Chadband and the rest of them—whatever they are, they must be all of it within narrow bounds, within the few scenes that can be allotted to them; and if one of them fails now and then it is not surprising, the wonder is that most of them succeed so brilliantly. In thus translating his picture into action Dickens chose the most exigent way, but it was always the right way for him. He was curiously incapable in the other; when occasionally he tries his hand at picture-making, in Thackeray's manner—attempting to summarize an impression of social life among the Veneerings, of official life among the Barnacles—his touch is wild indeed. Away from a definite episode in an hour prescribed he is seldom at ease.

But though the actual presentation is thus dramatic, his books are in fact examples of the pictured scene that opens and spreads very gradually, in order to make a valid world for a drama that could not be precipitated forthwith, a drama that would be naked romance if it stood by itself. Stevenson happened upon this point, with regard to Dickens, in devising the same method for a story of his own, The Wrecker, a book in which he too proposed to insinuate an abrupt and violent intrigue into credible, continuous life. He, of course, knew precisely what

he was doing—where Dickens followed, as I
suppose, an uncritical instinct; the purpose of
The Wrecker is clearly written upon it, and very
ingeniously carried out. But I doubt whether
Stevenson himself noticed that in all his work, or
nearly, he was using an artifice of the same kind.
He spoke of his habitual inclination towards the
story told in the first person as though it were a
chance preference, and he may not have perceived
how logically it followed from the subjects that
mostly attracted him. They were strongly
romantic, vividly dramatic; he never had
occasion to use the first person for the effect I
considered a while ago, its enhancement of a
plain narrative. I called it the first step towards
the dramatization of a story, and so it is in a book
like Esmond, a broadly pictured novel of manners. But it is more than this in a book like The
Master of Ballantrae, where the subject is a piece
of forcible, closely knit action. The value of rendering it as somebody's narrative, of placing it in
the mouth of a man who was there on the spot,
is in this book the value of working the drama
into a picture, of passing it through a man's
thought and catching his reflection of it. As the
picture in Esmond is enhanced, so the drama in
Ballantrae is toned and qualified by the method
of presentation. The same method has a different
effect, according to the subject upon which it is
used; as a splash of the same grey might darken
white surface and lighten a black. In Esmond
the use of the first person raises the book in

the direction of drama, in Ballantrae it thrusts the book in the other direction, towards the pictured impression. So it would seem; but perhaps it is a fine distinction that criticism can afford to pass by.

XV

As for the peculiar accent and stir of life, the life
behind the story, Balzac's manner of finding and
expressing it is always interesting. He seems to
look for it most readily, not in the nature of the
men and women whose action makes the story,
or not there to begin with, but in their streets
and houses and rooms. He cannot think of his
people without the homes they inhabit; with
Balzac to imagine a human being is to imagine a
province, a city, a corner of the city, a building
at a turn of the street, certain furnished rooms,
and finally the man or woman who lives in them.
He cannot be satisfied that the tenor of this
creature's existence is at all understood without
a minute knowledge of the things and objects that
surround it. So strong is his conviction upon this
point that it gives a special savour to the many
pages in which he describes how the doorway is
approached, how the passage leads to the staircase, how the parlour-chairs are placed, in the
house which is to be the scene of his drama.
These descriptions are clear and business-like;
they are offered as an essential preliminary to
the story, a matter that must obviously be dealt
with, once for all, before the story can proceed.
And he communicates his certainty to the reader,

THE CRAFT OF FICTION

he imposes his belief in the need for precision and fullness; Balzac is so sure that every detail *must* be known, down to the vases on the mantelpiece or the pots and pans in the cupboard, that his reader cannot begin to question it. Everything is made to appear as important as the author feels it to be.

His manner is well to be watched in Eugénie Grandet. That account of the great bare old house of the miser at Saumur is as plain and straightforward as an inventory; no attempt is made to insinuate the impression of the place by hints and side-lights. Balzac marches up to it and goes steadily through it, until our necessary information is complete, and there he leaves it. There is no subtlety in such a method, it seems; a lighter, shyer handling of the facts, more suggestion and less statement, might be expected to make a deeper effect. And indeed Balzac's confident way is not one that would give a good result in most hands; it would produce the kind of description that the eye travels over unperceivingly, the conscientious introduction that tells us nothing. Yet Balzac contrives to make it tell everything; and the simple explanation is that he, more than anyone else, *knows* everything. The place exists in his thought; it is not to him the mere sensation of a place, with cloudy corners, uncertain recesses, which only grow definite as he touches and probes them with his phrases. A writer of a different sort, an impressionist who is aware of the effect of a scene rather

than of the scene itself, proceeds inevitably
after another fashion; if he attempted Balzac's
method he would have to feel his way tentatively,
adding fact to fact, and his account would consist
of that mechanical sum of details which makes no
image. Balzac is so thoroughly possessed of his
image that he can reproduce it inch by inch, fact
by fact, without losing the effect of it as a whole;
he can start from the edge of his scene, from a
street of old houses, from the doorstep of one old
house, and leave a perfectly firm and telling
impression behind him as he proceeds. When his
description is finished and the last detail in its
place, the home of the Grandets is securely built
for the needs of the story, possessing all the
significance that Balzac demands of it.

It will presently be seen that he demands a
great deal. I said that his drama has always the
benefit of a reserve of force, stored up for it
beforehand in the general picture; and though in
this picture is included the fortunes and characters
of the men and women, of the Grandets and
their neighbours, a large part of it is the material
scene, the very walls that are to witness the
coming events. The figure of Grandet, the old
miser, is indeed called up and accounted for
abundantly, in all the conditions of his past; but
the house too, within and without, is laid under
strict contribution, is used to the full in the story.
It is a presence and an influence that counts
throughout—and counts particularly in a matter
that is essential to the book's effect, a matter

that could scarcely be provided for in any other way, as it happens. Of this I shall speak in a moment; but at once it is noticeable how the Maison Grandet, like the Maison Vauquer, helps the book on its way. It incarnates all the past of its old owner, and visibly links it to the action when the story opens. The elaborate summary of Grandet's early life, the scrupulously exact account of the building of his prosperity, is brought to an issue in the image of the " cold, dreary and silent house at the upper end of the town," from whence the drama widens again in its turn. How it is that Balzac has precisely the right scene in his mind, a house that perfectly expresses his *donnée* and all its associations—that, of course, is Balzac's secret; his method would be nothing without the quality of his imagination. His use of the scene is another matter, and there it is possible to reckon how much of his general effect, the sense of the moral and social foundation of his story, is given by its inanimate setting. He has to picture a character and a train of life, and to a great extent he does so by describing a house.

Beyond old Grandet and the kind of existence imposed upon his household, the drama needs little by way of preparation. The miser's daughter Eugénie, with her mother, must stand out clearly to the fore; but a very few touches bring these two women to life in their shadowy abode. They are simple and patient and devoted; between the dominance of the old man and the monotony

of the provincial routine Eugénie and her mother
are easily intelligible. The two local aspirants to
the girl's fortune, and their supporters on either
side—the Cruchotins and the Grassinistes—are
subsidiary figures; they are sufficiently rendered
by their appearance in a flock, for a sociable
evening with the Grandets. The faithful maid-
servant, the shrewd and valiant Nanon, is
quickly sketched. And there, then, is the picture
that Balzac prepares for the action, which opens
with the arrival of Charles, Eugénie's young and
unknown cousin. Except for Charles, all the
material of the drama is contained in the first
impression of the household and the small
country-town; Eugénie's story is implied in it;
and her romance, from the moment it begins,
inherits the reality and the continuity of the
experience. Charles himself is so light a weight
that in his case no introduction is needed at all;
a single glance at him is enough to show the
charm of his airy elegance. His only function in
the story is to create the long dream of Eugénie's
life; and for that he needs nothing but his
unlikeness to the Cruchotins and the Grassinistes.
They and Eugénie, therefore, between them,
provide for his effect before he appears, they by
their dull provinciality, she by her sensitive
ignorance. The whole scene, on the verge of the
action, is full of dormant echoes, and the first
movement wakes them. The girl placed as she is,
her circumstances known as they are, all but
make the tale of their own accord; only the

simple facts are wanting, their effect is already in the air.

And accordingly the story slips away from its beginning without hesitation. In a sense it is a very slight story; there is scarcely anything in it but Eugénie's quick flush of emotion, and then her patient cherishing of its memory; and this simplicity may seem to detract, perhaps, from the skilfulness of Balzac's preparation. Where there is so little in the way of incident or clash of character to provide for, where the people are so plain and perspicuous and next to nothing happens to them, it should not be difficult to make an expressive scene for the drama and its few facts. All that occurs in the main line of the story is that Eugénie falls in love with her cousin, bids him good-bye when he goes to make his fortune in the Indies, trustfully awaits him for a number of years, and discovers his faithlessness when he returns. Her mother's death, and then her father's, are almost the only events in the long interval of Charles's absence. Simple indeed, but this is exactly the kind of story which it is most puzzling to handle. The material is scanty, and yet it covers a good many years; and somehow the narrative must render the length of the years without the help of positive and concrete stuff to fill them. The whole point of the story is lost unless we are made to feel the slow crawling of time, while Eugénie waited; but what is there in her life to account for the time, to bridge the interval, to illustrate its extent?

Balzac has to make a long impression of vacuity; Eugénie Grandet contains a decidedly tough subject.

In such a case I suppose the first instinct of almost any story-teller would be to lengthen the narrative of her loneliness by elaborating the picture of her state of mind, drawing out the record of expectancy and patience and failing hope. If nothing befalls her from without, or so little, the time must be filled with the long drama of her experience within; the centre of the story would then be cast in her consciousness, in which there would be reflected the gradual drop of her emotion from glowing newness to the level of daily custom, and thence again to the chill of disillusion. It is easy to imagine the kind of form which the book would take. In order to assure its full value to Eugénie's monotonous suffering, the story would be given from her point of view, entirely from hers; the external facts of her existence would all be seen through her eyes. making substance for her thought. We should live *with* Eugénie, throughout; we should share her vigil, morning and evening, summer and winter, while she sat in the silent house and listened to the noises of life in the street, while the sun shone for others and not for her, while the light waned, the wind howled, the snow fell and hushed the busy town—still Eugénie would sit at her window, still we should follow the flow of her resigned and uncomplaining meditations; until at last the author could judge that five years, ten years, whatever it may be, had been sufficiently shown in their dreary lapse, and that Charles might now come back from the Indies. So it would be and so it would have to be, a novelist might easily feel. How else could the due suggestion of time be given, where there is so little to show for it in dramatic facts?

But Balzac's treatment of the story is quite unexpected. He lays it out in a fashion that is worth noting, as a good example of the freedom of movement that his great pictorial genius allowed him. With his scene and its general setting so perfectly rendered, the story takes care of itself on every side, with the minimum of trouble on his part. His real trouble is over when the action begins; he is not even disturbed by this difficulty of presenting the sense of time. The plan of Eugénie Grandet, as the book stands, seems to have been made without any regard to the chief and most exacting demand of the story; where another writer would be using every device he could think of to mark the effect of the succeeding years, Balzac is free to tell the story as straightforwardly as he chooses. To Eugénie the great and only adventure of her life was contained in the few days or weeks of Charles's first visit; nothing to compare with that excitement ever happened to her again. And Balzac makes this episode bulk as largely in the book as it did in her life; he pauses over it and elaborates it, unconcerned by the fact that in the book—in the whole effect it is to produce—the episode is only the beginning of Eugénie's story, only the prelude to her years of waiting and watching.

He extends his account of it so far, nevertheless, that he has written two thirds of the book by the time the young man is finally despatched to the Indies. It means that the duration of the story—and the duration is the principal fact in it—is hardly considered at all, after the opening of the action. There is almost no picture of the slowly moving years; there is little but a concise chronicle of the few widely spaced events. Balzac is at no pains to sit with Eugénie in the twilight, while the seasons revolve; not for him to linger, gazing sympathetically over her shoulder, tenderly exploring her sentiments. He is actually capable of beginning a paragraph with the casual announcement, " Five years went by in this way," as though he belonged to the order of story-tellers who imagine that time may be expressed by the mere statement of its length. Yet there is time in his book, it is very certain—time that lags and loiters till the girl has lost her youth and has dropped into the dull groove from which she will evidently never again be dislodged. Balzac can treat the story as concisely as he will, he can record Eugénie's simple experience from without, and yet make the fading of her young hope appear as gradual and protracted as need be; and all because he has prepared in advance, with his picture of the life of the Grandets, a complete and enduring impression.

His preliminary picture included the representation of time, secured the sense of it so thoroughly that there is no necessity for recurring to it again. The routine of the Maison Grandet is too clearly known to be forgotten; the sight of the girl and her mother, leading their sequestered lives in the shadow of their old tyrant's obsession, is a sensation that persists to the end of their story. Their dreary days accumulate and fill the year with hardly a break in its monotony; the next year and the next are the same, except that old Grandet's meanness is accentuated as his wealth increases; the present is like the past, the future will prolong the present. In such a scene Eugénie's patient acquiescence in middle age becomes a visible fact, is divined and accepted at once, without further insistence; it is latent in the scene from the beginning, even at the time of the small romance of her youth. To dwell upon the shades of her long disappointment is needless, for her power of endurance and her fidelity are fully created in the book before they are put to the test. " Five years went by," says Balzac; but before he says it we already see them opening and closing upon the girl, bearing down upon her solitude, exhausting her freshness but not the dumb resignation in which she sits and waits. The endlessness, the sameness, the silence, which another writer would have to tackle somehow after disposing of the brief episode of Charles's visit, Balzac has it all in hand, he can finish off his book without long delay. His deliberate approach to the action, through the picture of the house and its inmates, has achieved its purpose; it has given him the effect which the action most demands and could least acquire by itself, the effect of time.

And there is no doubt that the story immensely gains by being treated in Balzac's way, rather than as the life of a disappointed girl, studied from within. In that case the subject of the book might easily seem to be wearing thin, for the fact is that Eugénie has not the stuff of character to give much interest to her story, supposing it were seen through her eyes. She is good and true and devoted, but she lacks the poetry, the inner resonance, that might make a living drama of her simple emotions. Balzac was always too prosaic for the creation of virtue; his innocent people— unless they may be grotesque as well as innocent, like Pons or Goriot—live in a world that is not worth the trouble of investigation. The interest of Eugénie would infallibly be lowered, not heightened, by closer participation in her romance; it is much better to look at it from outside, as Balzac does for the most part, and to note the incidents that befell her, always provided that the image of lagging time can be fashioned and preserved. As for that, Balzac has no cause to be anxious; it is as certain that he can do what he will with the subject of a story, handle it aright and compel it to make its impression, as that he will fail to understand the sensibility of a good-natured girl.

I cannot imagine that the value of the novelist's

picture, as preparation for his drama, could be proved more strikingly than it is proved in this book, where so much is expected of it. Eugénie Grandet is typical of a natural bent on the part of any prudent writer of fiction, the instinct to relieve the climax of the story by taxing it as little as possible when it is reached. The climax ought to complete, to add the touch that makes the book whole and organic; that is its task, and that only. It should be free to do what it must without any unnecessary distraction, and nothing need distract it that can be dealt with and despatched at an earlier stage. The climax in Grandet is not a dramatic point, not a single incident; it lies in the slow chill that very gradually descends upon Eugénie's hope. Balzac carefully refrains from making the book hinge on anything so commonplace as a sudden discovery of the young man's want of faith. The worst kind of disappointment does not happen like that, falling as a stroke; it steals into a life and spreads imperceptibly. Charles's final act of disloyalty is only a kind of coda to a drama that is practically complete without it. Here, then, is a climax that is essentially pictorial, an impression of change and decay, needing time in plenty above all; and Balzac leads into it so cunningly that a short summary of a few plain facts is all that is required, when it comes to the point. He saves his climax, in other words, from the burden of deliberate expatiation, which at first sight it would seem bound to incur; he leaves nothing for it to accomplish but just the necessary touch, the movement that declares and fulfils the intention of the book.

There is the same power at work upon material even more baffling, apparently, in La Recherche de l'Absolu. The subject of that perfect tale is of course the growth of a fixed idea, and Balzac was faced with the task of showing the slow aggravation of a man's ruin through a series of outbreaks, differing in no way one from another, save in their increasing violence. Claes, the excellent and prosperous young burgher of Douai, pillar of the old civic stateliness of Flanders, is dragged and dragged into his calamitous experiments by the bare failure (as he is persuaded) of each one in turn ; each time his researches are on the verge of yielding him the " absolute," the philosopher's stone, and each time the prospect is more shining than before ; success, wealth enough to restore his deepening losses a thousand times over, is assured by one more attempt, the money to make it must be found. And so all other interest in life is forgotten, his pride and repute are sacrificed, the splendid house is gradually stripped of its treasures, his family are thrust into poverty ; and he himself dies degraded, insane, with success—surely, surely success, this time—actually in his grasp. That is all, and on that straight, sustained movement the book must remain throughout, re-iterating one effect with growing intensity— always at the pitch of high hope and sharp disappointment, always prepared to heighten and sharpen it a little further. There can be no development through any variety of incident; it is the same suspense and the same shock, again and again, constantly more disastrous than before.

Here, too, Balzac amasses in his opening picture the reserve of effect that he needs. He recognizes the ample resource of the dignity, the opulence, the worth, the tradition inherited by families like that of Claes—merchant-princes of honourable line, rulers of rich cities, patrons of great art. The house of Claes, with its fine architecture, its portraits, its dark furniture and gleaming silver, its garden of rare tulips— Balzac's imagination is poured into the scene, it is exactly the kind of opportunity that he welcomes. He knows the place by heart; his description of it is in his most methodical style. Steadily it all comes out, a Holbein-picture with every orderly detail duly arranged, the expression of good manners, sound taste and a solid position. On such a world, created as he knows how to create it, he may draw without hesitation for the repeated demands of the story; the protracted havoc wrought by the man's infatuation is represented, step by step, as the visible scene is denuded and destroyed. His spirit is worn away and his sanity breaks down, and the successive strokes that fall on it, instead of losing force (for the onlooker) by repetition, are renewed and increased by the sight of the spreading devastation around him, as his precious things are cast into the devouring expense of his researches. Their disappearance is the outward sign of his own personal surrender to his idea, and each time that he is thrown back upon disappointment the ravage of the scene in which he was placed at the beginning of the book is more evident than before. It spreads through his pictures and treasures to his family, and still further into his relations with the respectable circle about him. His position is shaken, his situation in that beautiful Holbein-world is undermined; it is slowly shattered as his madness extends. And having built and furnished that world so firmly and richly, Balzac can linger upon its overthrow as long as is necessary for the rising effect of his story. He has created so much that there is plenty to destroy; only at last, with the man's dying cry of triumph, is the wreck complete.

Thus the climax of the story, as in Grandet, is laid up betimes in the descriptive picture. It is needless, I suppose, to insist on the esthetic value of economy of this kind. Everybody feels the greater force of the climax that assumes its right place without an effort, when the time comes, compared with that in which a strain and an exaggerated stress are perceptible. The process of writing a novel seems to be one of continual forestalling and anticipating; far more important than the immediate page is the page to come, still in the distance, on behalf of which this one is secretly working. The writer makes a point and reserves it at the same time, creates an effect and holds it back, till in due course it is appropriated and used by the page for which it is intended. It must be a pleasure to the writer, it is certainly a great pleasure to the critic, when the stroke is cleanly brought off. It is the same pleasure indeed ; the novelist makes the stroke, but the critic makes it again by perceiving it, and is legitimately satisfied by the sense of having perceived it with good artistry. It is spoilt, of course, if the stroke is handled tactlessly and obtrusively ; the art of preparation is no art if it betrays itself at the outset, calling attention to its purpose. By definition it is unrecognizable until it attains its end ; it is the art of rendering an impression that is found to have been made, later on, but that evades detection at the moment. The particular variety I have been considering is one of which Balzac is a great master ; and perhaps his mastery will appear still more clearly if I look at a book in which his example is *not* followed in this respect. It is a finer book, for all that, than most of Balzac's.

XVI

I<small>T</small> is Anna Karenina; and I turn to it now, not
for its beauty and harmony, not because it is one
of the most exquisitely toned, shaded, gradated
pieces of portraiture in fiction, but because it
happens to show very clearly how an effect may
be lost for want of timely precaution. Tolstoy
undoubtedly damaged a magnificent book by his
refusal to linger over any kind of pictorial
introduction. There is none in this story, the
reader will remember. The whole of the book,
very nearly, is scenic, from the opening page to
the last; it is a chain of particular occasions,
acted out, talked out, by the crowd of people
concerned. Each of these scenes is outspread
before the spectator, who watches the characters
and listens to their dialogue; there is next to no
generalization of the story at any point. On every
page, I think, certainly on all but a very few of
the many hundred pages, the hour and the place
are exactly defined. Something is happening
there, or something is being discussed; at any
rate it is an episode singled out for direct vision.

The plan of the book, in fact, is strictly dramatic;
it allows no such freedom as Balzac uses, freedom
of exposition and retrospect. Tolstoy never draws
back from the immediate scene, to picture the

236

manner of life that his people led or to give a foreshortened impression of their history. He unrolls it all as it occurs, illustrating everything in action. It is an extraordinary feat, considering the amount of experience he undertakes to display, with an interweaving of so many lives and fortunes. And it is still more extraordinary, considering the nature of the story, which is not really dramatic at all, but a pictorial contrast, Anna and her affair on one side of it, Levin and his on the other. The contrast is gradually extended and deepened through the book; but it leads to no clash between the two, no opposition, no drama. It is an effect of slow and inevitable change, drawn out in minute detail through two lives, with all the others that cluster round each—exactly the kind of matter that nobody but Tolstoy, with his huge hand, would think of trying to treat scenically. Tolstoy so treats it, however, and apparently never feels any desire to break away from the march of his episodes or to fuse his swarming detail into a general view. It means that he must write a very long book, with scores and scores of scenes, but he has no objection to that.

It is only in its plan, of course, that Anna Karenina is strictly dramatic; its method of execution is much looser, and there indeed Tolstoy allows himself as much freedom as he pleases. In the novel of pure drama the point of view is that of the reader alone, as we saw; there is no " going behind " the characters, no direct revelation of their thought. Such consistency is out of the question, however, even for Tolstoy, on the great scale of his book; and he never hesitates to lay bare the mind of any of his people, at any moment, if it seems to help the force or the lucidity of the scene. And so we speedily grow familiar with the consciousness of many of them, for Tolstoy's hand is always as light and quick as it is broad. He catches the passing thought that is in a man's mind as he speaks; and though it may be no more than a vague doubt or an idle fancy, it is somehow a note of the man himself, a sign of his being, an echo of his inner tone. From Anna and the other figures of the forefront, down to the least of the population of the background, I could almost say to the wonderful little red baby that in one of the last chapters is disclosed to Levin by the triumphant nurse—each of them is a centre of vision, each of them looks out on a world that is not like the world of the rest, and we know it. Without any elaborate research Tolstoy expresses the nature of all their experience; he reveals the dull weight of it in one man's life or its vibrating interest in another's; he shows how for one it stirs and opens, with troubling enlargement, how for another it remains blank and inert. He does so unconsciously, it might seem, not seeking to construct the world as it appears to Anna or her husband or her lover, but simply glancing now and then into their mood of the moment, and indicating what he happens to find there. Yet

238

it is enough, and each of them is soon a human being whose privacy we share. They are actors moving upon a visible scene, watched from the reader's point of view; but they are also sentient lives, understood from within.

Here, then, is a mixed method which enables Tolstoy to deal with his immense subject on the lines of drama. He can follow its chronology step by step, at an even pace throughout, without ever interrupting the rhythm for that shift of the point of view—away from the immediate scene to a more commanding height—which another writer would certainly have found to be necessary sooner or later. He can create a character in so few words—he can make the manner of a man's or a woman's thought so quickly intelligible— that even though his story is crowded and over-crowded with people he can render them all, so to speak, by the way, give them all their due without any study of them outside the passing episode. So he can, at least, in general; for in Anna Karenina, as I said, his method seems to break down very conspicuously at a certain juncture. But before I come to that, I would dwell further upon this peculiar skill of Tolstoy's, this facility which explains, I think, the curious flaw in his beautiful novel. He would appear to have trusted his method too far, trusted it not only to carry him through the development and the climax of his story, but also to constitute his *donnée*, his prime situation in the beginning. This was to throw too much upon it, and it is critically

of high interest to see where it failed, and why.
The miscalculations of a great genius are enlightening; here, in Anna Karenina, is one that
calls attention to Tolstoy's characteristic fashion
of telling a story, and declares its remarkable
qualities.

The story of Anna, I suggested, is not essentially dramatic. Like the story of Emma Bovary
or of Eugénie Grandet, it is a picture outspread,
an impression of life, rather than an action. Anna
at first has a life that rests on many supports,
with her husband and her child and her social
possessions; it is broadly based and its stability
is assured, if she chooses to rely on it. But her
husband is a dull and pedantic soul, and before
long she chooses to exchange her assured life for
another that rests on one support only, a romantic
passion. Her life with Vronsky has no other
security, and in process of time it fails. Its
gradual failure is her story—the losing battle of
a woman who has thrown away more resources
than she could afford. But the point and reason
of the book is not in the dramatic question—
what will happen, will Anna lose or win? It is in
the picture of her gathering and deepening
difficulties, difficulties that arise out of her
position and her mood, difficulties of which the
only solution is at last her death. And this story,
with the contrasted picture of Levin's domesticity
that completes it, is laid out exactly as Balzac
did *not* lay out his story of Eugénie; it is all
presented as action, because Tolstoy's eye was

infallibly drawn, whenever he wrote, to the instant aspect of his matter, the play itself. He could not generalize it, and on the whole there was no need for him to do so; for there was nothing, not the least stir of motive or character, that could not be expressed in the movement of the play as he handled it. Scene is laid to scene, therefore, as many as he requires; he had no thought of stinting himself in that respect. And within the limit of the scene he was always ready to vary his method, to enter the consciousness of any or all the characters at will, without troubling himself about the possible confusion of effect which this might entail. He could afford the liberty, because the main lines of his structure were so simple and clear; the inconsistencies of his method are dominated by the broad scenic regularity of his plan.

Balzac had not the master-hand of Tolstoy in the management of a dramatic scene, an episode. When it comes to rendering a piece of action Balzac's art is not particularly felicitous, and if we only became acquainted with his people while they are talking and acting, I think they might often seem rather heavy and wooden, harsh of speech and gesture. Balzac's *general* knowledge of them, and his power of offering an impression of what he knows—these are so great that his people are alive before they begin to act, alive with an energy that is all-sufficient. Tolstoy's grasp of a human being's whole existence, of everything that goes to make it, is not as capacious as Balzac's; but on the other hand he can create a living scene, exquisitely and easily expressive, out of anything whatever, the lightest trifle of an incident. If he describes how a child lingered at the foot of the stairs, teasing an old servant, or how a peasant-woman stood in a doorway, laughing and calling to the men at work in the farmyard, the thing becomes a poetic event; in half a page he makes an unforgetable scene. It suddenly glows and flushes, and its effect in the story is profound. A passing glimpse of this kind is caught, say, by Anna in her hungry desperation, by Levin as he wanders and speculates; and immediately their experience is the fuller by an eloquent memory. The vividness of the small scene becomes a part of them, for us who read; it is something added to our impression of their reality. And so the half-page is not a diversion or an interlude; it speeds the story by augmenting the tone and the value of the lives that we are watching. It happens again and again; that is Tolstoy's way of creating a life, of raising it to its full power by a gradual process of enrichment, till Anna or Levin is at length a complete being, intimately understood, ready for the climax of the tale.

But of course it takes time, and it chanced that this deliberation made a special difficulty in the case of Anna's story. As for Levin, it was easy to give him ample play; he could be left to emerge and to assume his place in the book by leisurely degrees, for it is not until much has passed that his full power is needed. Meanwhile he is a figure in the crowd, a shy and disappointed suitor, unobtrusively sympathetic, and there are long opportunities of seeing more of him in his country solitude. Later on, when his fortunes come to the front with his marriage, he has shown what he is; he steps fully fashioned into the drama. With Anna it is very different; her story allows no such pause, for a growing knowledge of the manner of woman she may be. She is at once to the front of the book; the situation out of which the whole novel develops is made by a particular crisis in her life. She meets and falls in love with Vronsky—that is the crisis from which the rest of her story proceeds; it is the beginning of the action, the subject of the earliest chapters. And the difficulty lies in this, that she must be represented upon such a critical height of emotion before there is time, by Tolstoy's method, to create the right effect for her and to make her impulse really intelligible. For the reader it is all too abrupt, the step by which she abandons her past and flings herself upon her tragic adventure. It is impossible to measure her passion and her resolution, because she herself is still incompletely rendered. She has appeared in a few charming scenes, a finished and graceful figure, but that is not enough. If she is so soon to be seen at this pitch of exaltation, it is essential that her life should be fully shared by the onlooker; but as Tolstoy has told the story, Anna is in the midst of her crisis and has passed it before it is possible to know her life clearly from within. Alive and beautiful she is from the very first moment of her appearance; Tolstoy's art is much too sure to miss the right effect, so far as it goes. And if her story were such that it involved her in no great adventure at the start— if she could pass from scene to scene, like Levin, quietly revealing herself—Tolstoy's method would be perfect. But as it is, there is no adequate preparation; Anna is made to act as a deeply stirred and agitated woman before she has the *value* for such emotions. She has not yet become a presence familiar enough, and there is no means of gauging the force of the storm that is seen to shake her.

It is a flaw in the book which has often been noticed, and it is a flaw which Tolstoy could hardly have avoided, if he was determined to hold to his scenic plan. Given his reluctance to leave the actually present occasion, from the first page onwards, from the moment Anna's erring brother wakes to his own domestic troubles at the opening of the book, there is not room for the due creation of Anna's life. Her turning-point must be reached without delay, it cannot be deferred, for it is there that the development of the book begins. All that precedes her union with Vronsky is nothing but the opening stage, the matter that must be displayed before the story can begin to expand. The story, as we have seen, is in the picture of Anna's life *after* her critical choice, so that the first part of the book, the account of the given situation, cannot extend its limits. If, therefore, the situation is to be really made and constituted, the space it may cover must be tightly packed; the method should be that which most condenses and concentrates the representation. A great deal is to be expressed at once, all Anna's past and present, the kind of experience that has made her and that has brought her to the point she now touches. Without this her action is arbitrary and meaningless; it is vain to say that she acted thus and thus unless we perfectly understand what she was, what she had, what was around her, in the face of her predicament. Obviously there is no space to lose; and it is enough to look at Tolstoy's use of it, and then to see how Balzac makes the situation that *he* requires—the contrast shows exactly where Tolstoy's method could not help him. His refusal to shape his story, or any considerable part of it, as a pictorial impression, his desire to keep it all in immediate action, prevents him from making the most of the space at his command; the situation is bound to suffer in consequence.

For suppose that Balzac had had to deal with the life of Anna. He would certainly have been in no hurry to plunge into the action, he would have felt that there was much to treat before the scene was ready to open. All the initial episodes of Tolstoy's book, from Anna's first appearance until she drops into Vronsky's arms, Balzac might well have ignored entirely. He would have

245

been too busy with his prodigious summary of the history and household of the Karenins to permit himself a glance in the direction of any particular moment, until the story could unfold from a situation thoroughly prepared. If Tolstoy had followed this course we should have lost some enchanting glimpses, but Balzac would have left not a shadow of uncertainty in the matter of Anna's disastrous passion. He would have shown precisely how she was placed in the conditions of her past, how she was exposed to this new incursion from without, and how it broke up a life which had satisfied her till then. He would have started his action in due time with his whole preliminary effect completely rendered; there would be no more question of it, no possibility that it would prove inadequate for the sequel. And all this he would have managed, no doubt, in fewer pages than Tolstoy needs for the beautiful scenes of his earlier chapters, scenes which make a perfect impression of Anna and her circle as an onlooker might happen to see them, but which fail to give the onlooker the kind of intimacy that is needed. Later on, indeed, her life is penetrated to the depths; but then it is too late to save the effect of the beginning. To the very end Anna is a wonderful woman whose early history has never been fully explained. The facts are clear, of course, and there is nothing impossible about them; but her passion for this man, the grand event of her life, has to be assumed on the word of the author. All that he really showed, to start with, was a slight, swift love-story, which might have ended as easily as it began.

The method of the book, in short, does not arise out of the subject; in treating it Tolstoy simply used the method that was congenial to him, without regarding the story that he had to tell. He began it as though Anna's break with her past was the climax to which the story was to mount, whereas it is really the point from which the story sets out for its true climax in her final catastrophe. And so the first part of the book is neither one thing nor the other; it is not an independent drama, for it cannot reach its height through all the necessary sweep of development; and on the other hand it is not a sufficient preparation for the great picture of inevitable disaster which is to follow. Tolstoy doubtless counted on his power—and not without reason, for it is amazing—to call people into life by means of a few luminous episodes; he knew he could make a living creature of Anna by bringing her into view in half a dozen scenes. She descends, accordingly, upon her brother's agitated household like a beneficent angel, she shines resplendent at some social function, she meets Vronsky, she talks to her husband; and Tolstoy is right, she becomes a real and exquisite being forthwith. But he did not see how much more was needed than a simple personal impression of her, in view of all that is to come. Not she only, but her world, the world as she sees it, her past as it

THE CRAFT OF FICTION

affects her—this too is demanded, and for this
he makes no provision. It is never really shown
how she was placed in her life, and what it
meant to her; and her flare of passion has
consequently no importance, no fateful bigness.
There is not enough of her, as yet, for such a
crisis.

It is not because Vronsky seems an inadequate
object of her passion; though it is true that with
the figure of Vronsky Tolstoy was curiously
unsuccessful. Vronsky was his one failure—
there is surely no other in all his gallery to match
it. The spoilt child of the world, but a friendly
soul, and a romantic and a patient lover—and a
type fashioned by conditions that Tolstoy, of
course, knew by heart—why should Tolstoy
manage to make so little of him? It is unfortunate, for when Anna is stirred by the sight of
him and his all-conquering speciosity, any reader
is sure to protest. Tolstoy should have created
Vronsky with a more certain touch before he
allowed him to cause such a disturbance. But
this is a minor matter, and it would count for
little if the figure of Anna were all it should be.
Vronsky's importance in the story is his importance to Anna, and her view of him is a part of
her; and he might be left lightly treated on his
own account, the author might be content to
indicate him rather summarily, so long as Anna
had full attention. It returns upon that again;
if Anna's own life were really fashioned, Vronsky's
effect would be *there*, and the independent effect

he happens to make, or to fail to make, on the reader would be an irrelevant affair. Tolstoy's vital failure is not with him, but with her, in the prelude of his book.

It may be that there is something of the same kind to be seen in another of his novels, in Resurrection, though Resurrection is more like a fragment of an epic than a novel. It cannot be said that in that tremendous book Tolstoy pictured the rending of a man's soul by sudden enlightenment, striking in upon him unexpectedly, against his will, and destroying his established life—and that is apparently the subject in the author's mind. It is the woman, the accidental woman through whom the stroke is delivered, who is actually in the middle of the book; it is *her* epic much rather than the man's, and Tolstoy did not succeed in placing him where he clearly meant him to be. The man's conversion from the selfishness of his commonplace prosperity is not much more than a fact assumed at the beginning of the story. It happens, Tolstoy says it happens, and the man's life is changed; and thereafter the sombre epic proceeds. But the unrolling of the story has no bearing upon the revolution wrought in the man; that is complete, as soon as he flings over his past and follows the convoy of prisoners into Siberia, and the succession of strange scenes has nothing more to accomplish in him. The man is the mirror of the scenes, his own drama is finished. And if Tolstoy intended to write the drama of a soul, all this presentation of the deadly journey into exile, given with the full force of his genius, is superfluous; his subject lay further back. But Resurrection, no doubt, *is* a fragment, a wonderful shifting of scenes that never reached a conclusion; and it is not to be criticized as a book in which Tolstoy tried and failed to carry out his purpose. I only mention it because it seems to illustrate, like Anna Karenina, his instinctive evasion of the matter that could not be thrown into straightforward scenic form, the form in which his imagination was evidently happiest. His great example, therefore, is complementary to that of Balzac, whose genius looked in the other direction, who was always drawn to the general picture rather than to the particular scene. And with these two illustrious names I reach the end of the argument I have tried to follow from book to book, and it is time to gather up the threads.

XVII

THE whole intricate question of method, in the craft of fiction, I take to be governed by the question of the point of view—the question of the relation in which the narrator stands to the story. He tells it as *he* sees it, in the first place; the reader faces the story-teller and listens, and the story may be told so vivaciously that the presence of the minstrel is forgotten, and the scene becomes visible, peopled with the characters of the tale. It may be so, it very often is so for a time. But it is not so always, and the story-teller himself grows conscious of a misgiving. If the spell is weakened at any moment, the listener is recalled from the scene to the mere author before him, and the story rests only upon the author's direct assertion. Is it not possible, then, to introduce another point of view, to set up a fresh narrator to bear the brunt of the reader's scrutiny? If the story-teller is *in* the story himself, the author is dramatized; his assertions gain in weight, for they are backed by the presence of the narrator in the pictured scene. It is advantage scored; the author has shifted his responsibility, and it now falls where the reader can see and measure it; the arbitrary quality which may at any time be detected in the author's voice is disguised in the voice of his spokesman. Nothing is now imported into the story from without; it is self-contained, it has no associations with anyone beyond its circle.

Such is the first step towards dramatization, and in very many a story it may be enough. The spokesman is there, in recognizable relation with his matter; no question of his authority can arise. But now a difficulty may be started by the nature of the tale that he tells. If he has nothing to do but to relate what he has seen, what any-one might have seen in his position, his account will serve very well; there is no need for more. Let him unfold his chronicle as it appears in his memory. But if he is himself the subject of his story, if the story involves a searching explora-tion of his own consciousness, an account in his own words, after the fact, is not by any means the best imaginable. Far better it would be to see him while his mind is actually at work in the agitation, whatever it may be, which is to make the book. The matter would then be objective and visible to the reader, instead of reaching him in the form of a report at second hand. But how to manage this without falling back upon the author and *his* report, which has already been tried and for good reasons, as it seemed, aban-doned? It is managed by a kind of repetition of the same stroke, a further shift of the point of view. The spectator, the listener, the reader, is now himself to be placed at the angle of vision; not an account or a report, more or less convincing, is to be offered him, but a direct sight of the matter itself, while it is passing. Nobody expounds or explains; the story is enacted by its look and behaviour at particular moments. By the first stroke the narrator was brought into the book and set before the reader; but the action appeared only in his narrative. Now the action is there, proceeding while the pages are turned; the narrator is forestalled, he is watched while the story is in the making. Such is the progress of the writer of fiction towards drama; such is his method of evading the drawbacks of a mere reporter and assuming the advantages, as far as possible, of a dramatist. How far he may choose to push the process in his book—that is a matter to be decided by the subject; it entirely depends upon the kind of effect that the theme demands. It may respond to all the dramatization it can get, it may give all that it has to give for less. The subject dictates the method.

And now let the process be reversed, let us start with the purely dramatic subject, the story that will tell itself in perfect rightness, unaided, to the eye of the reader. This story never deviates from a strictly scenic form; one occasion or episode follows another, with no interruption for any reflective summary of events. Necessarily it must be so, for it is only while the episode is proceeding that no question of a narrator can arise; when the scene closes the play ceases till the opening of the next. To glance upon the story from a height and to give a general impression of

THE CRAFT OF FICTION

its course—this is at once to remove the point of view from the reader and to set up a new one somewhere else; the method is no longer consistent, no longer purely dramatic. And the dramatic story is not only scenic, it is also limited to so much as the ear can hear and the eye see. In rigid drama of this kind there is naturally no admission of the reader into the private mind of any of the characters; their thoughts and motives are transmuted into action. A subject wrought to this pitch of objectivity is no doubt given weight and compactness and authority in the highest degree; it is like a piece of modelling, standing in clear space, casting its shadow. It is the most finished form that fiction can take.

But evidently it is not a form to which fiction can aspire in general. It implies many sacrifices, and these will easily seem to be more than the subject can usefully make. It is out of the question, of course, wherever the main burden of the story lies within some particular consciousness, in the study of a soul, the growth of a character, the changing history of a temperament; there the subject would be needlessly crossed and strangled by dramatization pushed to its limit. It is out of the question, again, wherever the story is too big, too comprehensive, too widely ranging, to be treated scenically, with no opportunity for general and panoramic survey; it has been discovered, indeed, that even a story of this kind *may* fall into a long succession of definite scenes, under some hands, but it has

also appeared that in doing so it incurs unnecessary disabilities, and will likely suffer.
These stories, therefore, which will not naturally
accommodate themselves to the reader's point of
view, and the reader's alone, we regard as rather
pictorial than dramatic—meaning that they call
for some narrator, somebody who *knows*, to
contemplate the facts and create an impression
of them. Whether it is the omniscient author or
a man in the book, he must gather up his experience, compose a vision of it as it exists in his
mind, and lay *that* before the reader. It is the
reflection of an experience; and though there
may be all imaginable diversity of treatment
within the limits of the reflection, such is its
essential character. In a pictorial book the
principle of the structure involves a point of view
which is not the reader's.

It is open to the pictorial book, however, to
use a method in its picture-making that is really
no other than the method of drama. It is somebody's experience, we say, that is to be reported,
the general effect that many things have left
upon a certain mind; it is a fusion of innumerable
elements, the deposit of a lapse of time. The
straightforward way to render it would be for the
narrator—the author or his selected creature—
to view the past retrospectively and discourse
upon it, to recall and meditate and summarize.
That is picture-making in its natural form, using
its own method. But exactly as in drama the
subject is distributed among the characters and

enacted by them, so in picture the effect may be entrusted to the elements, the reactions of the moment, and *performed* by these. The mind of the narrator becomes the stage, his voice is no longer heard. His voice *is* heard so long as there is narrative of any sort, whether he is speaking in person or is reported obliquely; his voice is heard, because in either case the language and the intonation are his, the direct expression of his experience. In the drama of his mind there is no personal voice, for there is no narrator; the point of view becomes the reader's once more. The shapes of thought in the man's mind tell their own story. And that is the art of picture-making when it uses the dramatic method.

But it cannot always do so. Constantly it must be necessary to offer the reader a summary of facts, an impression of a train of events, that can only be given as somebody's narration. Suppose it were required to render the general effect of a certain year in a man's life, a year that has filled his mind with a swarm of many memories. Looking into his consciousness after the year has gone, we might find much there that would indicate the nature of the year's events without any word on his part; the flickers and flashes of thought from moment to moment might indeed tell us much. But we shall need an account from him too, no doubt; too much has happened in a year to be wholly acted, as I call it, in the movement of the man's thought. He must narrate—he must make, that is to say, a picture of the events as he sees them, glancing back. Now if he speaks in the first person there can, of course, be no uncertainty in the point of view; he has his fixed position, he cannot leave it. His description will represent the face that the facts in their sequence turned towards *him*; the field of vision is defined with perfect distinctness, and his story cannot stray outside it. The reader, then, may be said to watch a reflection of the facts in a mirror of which the edge is nowhere in doubt; it is rounded by the bounds of the narrator's own personal experience.

This limitation may have a convenience and a value in the story, it may contribute to the effect. But it need not be forfeited, it is clear, if the first person is changed to the third. The author may use the man's field of vision and keep as faithfully within it as though the man were speaking for himself. In that case he retains this advantage and adds to it another, one that is likely to be very much greater. For now, while the point of view is still fixed in space, still assigned to the man in the book, it is free in *time*; there no longer stretches, between the narrator and the events of which he speaks, a certain tract of time, across which the past must appear in a more or less distant perspective. All the variety obtainable by a shifting relation to the story in time is thus in the author's hand; the safe serenity of a far retrospect, the promising or threatening urgency of the present, every gradation between the two, can be drawn into the whole effect of the

book, and all of it without any change of the
seeing eye. It is a liberty that may help the story
indefinitely, raising this matter into strong relief,
throwing that other back into vaguer shade.

And next, still keeping mainly and ostensibly
to the same point of view, the author has the
chance of using a much greater latitude than he
need appear to use. The seeing eye is with somebody in the book, but its vision is reinforced; the
picture contains more, becomes richer and fuller,
because it is the author's as well as his creature's,
both at once. Nobody notices, but in fact there
are now two brains behind that eye; and one of
them is the author's, who adopts and shares the
position of his creature, and at the same time
supplements his wit. If you analyse the picture
that is now presented, you find that it is not all
the work of the personage whose vision the
author has adopted. There are touches in it that
go beyond any sensation of his, and indicate that
some one else is looking over his shoulder—seeing
things from the same angle, but seeing more,
bringing another mind to bear upon the scene.
It is an easy and natural extension of the personage's power of observation. The impression of
the scene may be deepened as much as need be;
it is not confined to the scope of one mind, and
yet there is no blurring of the focus by a double
point of view. And thus what I have called the
sound of the narrator's voice (it is impossible to
avoid this mixture of metaphors) is less insistent
in oblique narration, even while it seems to be

following the very same argument that it would in direct, because another voice is speedily mixed and blended with it.

So this is another resource upon which the author may draw according to his need; sometimes it will be indispensable, and generally, I suppose, it will be useful. It means that he keeps a certain hold upon the narrator *as an object*; the sentient character in the story, round whom it is grouped, is not utterly subjective, completely given over to the business of seeing and feeling on behalf of the reader. It is a considerable point; for it helps to meet one of the great difficulties in the story which is carefully aligned towards a single consciousness and consistently so viewed. In that story the man or woman who acts as the vessel of sensation is always in danger of seeming a light, uncertain weight compared with the other people in the book—simply because the other people are objective images, plainly outlined, while the seer in the midst is precluded from that advantage, and must see without being directly seen. He, who doubtless ought to bulk in the story more massively than any one, tends to remain the least recognizable of the company, and even to dissolve in a kind of impalpable blur. By his method (which I am supposing to have been adopted in full strictness) the author is of course forbidden to look this central figure in the face, to describe and discuss him; the light cannot be turned upon him immediately. And very often we see the method becoming an embarrassment to the author in consequence, and the devices by which he tries to mitigate it, and to secure some reflected sight of the seer, may even be tiresomely obvious. But the resource of which I speak is of a finer sort.

It gives to the author the power of imperceptibly edging away from the seer, leaving his consciousness, ceasing to use his eyes—though still without substituting the eyes of another. To revert for a moment to the story told in the first person, it is plain that in that case the narrator has no such liberty; his own consciousness must always lie open; the part that he plays in the story can never appear in the same terms, on the same plane, as that of the other people. Though he is not visible in the story to the reader, as the others are, he is at every moment *nearer* than they, in his capacity of the seeing eye, the channel of vision; nor can he put off his function, he must continue steadily to see and to report. But when the author is reporting *him* there is a margin of freedom. The author has not so completely identified himself, as narrator, with his hero that he can give him no objective weight whatever. If necessary he can allow him something of the value of a detached and phenomenal personage, like the rest of the company in the story, and that without violating the principle of his method. He cannot make his hero actually visible—there the method is uncompromising; he cannot step forward, leaving the man's point of view, and picture him from without. But he can place the man at the same distance from the reader as the other people, he can almost lend him the same effect, he can make of him a dramatic actor upon the scene.

And how? Merely by closing (when it suits him) the open consciousness of the seer—which he can do without any look of awkwardness or violence, since it conflicts in no way with the rule of the method. That rule only required that the author, having decided to share the point of view of his character, should not proceed to set up another of his own; it did not debar him from allowing his hero's act of vision to lapse, his function as the sentient creature in the story to be intermitted. The hero (I call him so for convenience—he may, of course, be quite a subordinate onlooker in the story) can at any moment become impenetrable, a human being whose thought is sealed from us; and it may seem a small matter, but in fact it has the result that he drops into the plane of the people whom he has hitherto been seeing and judging. Hitherto subjective, communicative in solitude, he has been in a category apart from them; but now he may mingle with the rest, engage in talk with them, and his presence and his talk are no more to the fore than theirs. As soon as some description or discussion of them is required, then, of course, the seer must resume his part and unseal his mind; but meanwhile, though the reader gets no direct view of him, still he is there in the dialogue with the rest, his speech (like theirs) issues from a hidden mind and has the same dramatic value. It is enough, very likely, to harden our image of him, to give precision to his form, to save him from dissipation into that luminous blur of which I spoke just now. For the author it is a resource to be welcomed on that account, and not on that account alone.

For besides the greater definition that the seer acquires, thus detached from us at times and relegated to the plane of his companions, there is much benefit for the subject of the story. In the tale that is quite openly and nakedly somebody's narrative there is this inherent weakness, that a scene of true drama is impossible. In true drama nobody *reports* the scene; it *appears*, it is constituted by the aspect of the occasion and the talk and the conduct of the people. When one of the people who took part in it sets out to report the scene, there is at once a mixture and a confusion of effects; for his own contribution to the scene has a different quality from the rest, cannot have the same crispness and freshness, cannot strike in with a new or unexpected note. This weakness may be well disguised, and like everything else in the whole craft it may become a positive and right effect in a particular story, for a particular purpose; it is always there, however, and it means that the full and unmixed effect of drama is denied to the story that is rigidly told from the point of view of one of the actors. But when that point of view is held in the manner I have described, when it is open to the author to withdraw from it silently and to leave the actor to play his part, true drama—or something so like it that it passes for true drama —is always possible; all the figures of the scene are together in it, one no nearer than another. Nothing is wanting save only that direct, un-equivocal sight of the hero which the method does indeed absolutely forbid.

Finally there is the old, immemorial, unguarded, unsuspicious way of telling a story, where the author entertains the reader, the minstrel draws his audience round him, the listeners rely upon his word. The voice is then confessedly and alone the author's; he imposes no limitation upon his freedom to tell what he pleases and to regard his matter from a point of view that is solely his own. And if there is anyone who can proceed in this fashion without appearing to lose the least of the advantages of a more cautious style, for him the minstrel's licence is proper and appropriate; there is no more to be said. But we have yet to discover him; and it is not very presumptuous in a critic, as things are, to declare that a story will never yield its best to a writer who takes the easiest way with it. He curtails his privileges and chooses a narrower method, and immediately the story responds; its better condition is too notable to be forgotten, when once it has caught the attention of a reader. The advantages that it gains are not nameless, indefinable graces, pleasing to a critic but impossible to fix in words; they are solid, we can describe and recount them.

And I can only conclude that if the novel is still as full of energy as it seems to be, and is not a form of imaginative art that, having seen the best of its day, is preparing to give place to some other, the novelist will not be willing to miss the inexhaustible opportunity that lies in its treatment. The easy way is no way at all; the only way is that by which the most is made of the story to be told, and the most was never made of any story except by a choice and disciplined method.

XVIII

In these pages I have tried to disengage the
various elements of the craft, one from another,
and to look at them separately; and this has
involved much rude simplification of matters that
are by no means simple. I have chosen a novel
for the sake of some particular aspect, and I have
disregarded all else in it; I could but seek for the
book which seemed to display that aspect most
plainly, and keep it in view from that one angle
for illustration of my theme. And the result is,
no doubt, that while some tentative classification
of the ways of a novelist has been possible, the
question that now arises, at the point I have
reached, must be left almost untouched. It is the
question that confronts a writer when he has possessed himself of his subject and determined the
point of view from which it is to be approached.
How is its development to be handled? Granted
that the instruments of the craft, dramatic and
pictorial and so forth, are such as they have been
described, which of them is the appropriate one for
this or that stage in the progress of the story to
be told? The point of view gives only a general
indication, deciding the look that the story is to
wear as a whole; but whether the action is to run

THE CRAFT OF FICTION

scenically, or to be treated on broader lines, or both—in short, the matter of the treatment in detail is still unsettled, though the main look and attitude of the book has been fixed by its subject.

My analysis of the making of a few novels would have to be pushed very much further before it would be possible to reach more than one or two conclusions in this connection. In the handling of his book a novelist must have some working theory, I suppose, to guide him—some theory of the relative uses and values of the different means at his disposal; and yet, when it is discovered how one writer tends perpetually towards one mode of procedure, another to another, it hardly seems that between them they have arrived at much certainty. Each employs the manner that is most congenial to him; nobody, it may be, gives us the material for elaborating the hierarchy of values that now we need, if this argument is to be extended. We have picked out the modes of rendering a story and have seen how they differ from each other; but we are not nearly in a position to give a reasoned account of their conjunction, how each is properly used in the place where its peculiar strength is required, how the course of a story demands one here, another there, as it proceeds to its culmination. I can imagine that by examining and comparing in detail the workmanship of many novels by many hands a critic might arrive at a number of inductions in regard to the relative properties of the scene, the incident dramatized, the incident pictured, the panoramic impression and the rest; there is scope for a large enquiry, the results of which are greatly needed by a critic of fiction, not to speak of the writers of it. The few books that I have tried to take to pieces and to reconstruct are not enough—or at least it would be necessary to deal with them more searchingly. But such slight generalizations as I have chanced upon by the way may as well be re-stated here, before I finish.

And first of the dramatic incident, the scene, properly so called—this comes first in importance, beyond doubt. A novelist instinctively sees the chief turns and phases of his story expressed in the form of a thing acted, where narrative ceases and a direct light falls upon his people and their doings. It must be so, for this is the sharpest effect within his range; and the story must naturally have the benefit of it, wherever the emphasis is to fall most strongly. To the scene, therefore, all other effects will appear to be subordinated in general; and the placing of the scenes of the story will be the prime concern. But precisely because it has this high value it will need to be used prudently. If it is wasted it loses force, and if it is weakened the climax—of the story, of a particular turn in the story—has no better resource to turn to instead. And so it is essential to recognize its limitations and to note the purposes which it does *not* well serve; since it is by using it for these that it is depreciated.

In the scene, it is clear, there can be no foreshortening of time or space; I mean that as it appears to the eye of the reader, it displays the whole of the time and space it occupies. It cannot cover more of either than it actually renders. And therefore it is, for its length, expensive in the matter of time and space; an oblique narrative will give the effect of further distances and longer periods with much greater economy. A few phrases, casting backwards over an incident, will yield the sense of its mere dimensions, where the dramatized scene might cover many pages. Its salience is another matter; but it has to be remembered that though the scene acts vividly, it acts slowly, in relation to its length. I am supposing that it stands alone and unsupported, and must accordingly make its effect from the beginning, must prepare as well as achieve; and evidently in that case a burden is thrown upon it for which it is not specially equipped. At any moment there may be reasons for forcing it to bear the burden—other considerations may preponderate; but nevertheless a scene which is not in some way prepared in advance is a scene which in point of fact is wasting a portion of its strength. It is accomplishing expensively what might have been accomplished for less.

That is the disability of the dramatic scene; and I imagine the novelist taking thought to ensure that he shall press upon it as little as possible. As far as may be he will use the scene for the purpose which it fulfils supremely—to

clinch a matter already pending, to demonstrate
a result, to crown an effect half-made by other
means. In that way he has all the help of its
strength without taxing its weakness. He secures
its salient relief, and by saving it from the necessity of doing all the work he enables it to act
swiftly and sharply. And then the scene exhibits
its value without drawback; it becomes a power
in a story that is entirely satisfying, and a thing
of beauty that holds the mind of the reader like
nothing else. It has often seemed that novelists
in general are over-shy of availing themselves of
this opportunity. They squander the scene; they
are always ready to break into dialogue, into
dramatic presentation, and often when there is
nothing definitely to be gained by it; but they
neglect the fully wrought and unified scene,
amply drawn out and placed where it gathers
many issues together, showing their outcome.
Such a scene, in which every part of it is active,
advancing the story, and yet in which there is no
forced effort, attempting a task not proper to it,
is a rare pleasure to see in a book. One immediately thinks of Bovary, and how the dramatic
scenes mark and affirm the structural lines of
that story.

Drama, then, gives the final stroke, it is the
final stroke which it is adapted to deliver; and
picture is to be considered as subordinate, preliminary and preparatory. This seems a plain
inference, on the whole, from all the books I have
been concerned with, not Bovary only. Picture,

the general survey, with its command of time and space, finds its opportunity where a long reach is more needed than sharp visibility. It is entirely independent where drama is circumscribed. It travels over periods and expanses, to and fro, pausing here, driving off into the distance there, making no account of the bounds of a particular occasion, but seeking its material wherever it chooses. Its office is to pile up an accumulated impression that will presently be completed by another agency, drama, which lacks what picture possesses, possesses what it lacks. Something of this kind, broadly speaking, is evidently their relation; and it is to be expected that a novelist will hold them to their natural functions, broadly speaking, in building his book. It is only a rough contrast, of course, the first and main difference between them that strikes the eye; comparing them more closely, one might find other divergences that would set their relation in a new light. But closer comparison is what I have not attempted; much more material would have to be collected and studied before it could begin.

Of the art of picture there is more to be said, however. It has appeared continually how the novelist is conscious of the thinness of a mere pictorial report of things; for thin and flat must be the reflection that we receive from the mind of another. There is a constant effort throughout the course of fiction to counteract the inherent weakness of this method of picture, the method that a story-teller is bound to use and that indeed is peculiarly his; and after tracing the successive stages of the struggle, in that which I have taken to be their logical order, we may possibly draw the moral. The upshot seems to be this—that the inherent weakness is to be plainly admitted and recognized, and not only that, but asserted and emphasized—and that then it ceases to be a weakness and actually becomes a new kind of strength. Is not this the result that we have seen? When you recall and picture an impression in words you give us, listeners and readers, no more than a sight of things in a mirror, not a direct view of them; but at the same time there is something of which you do indeed give us a direct view, as we may say, and that is the mirror, your mind itself. Of the mirror, then, you may make a solid and defined and visible object; you may dramatize this thing at least, this mind, if the things that appear in it must remain as pictures only. And so by accepting and using what looked like a mere disability in the method, you convert it into a powerful and valuable arm, with a keen effect of its own.

That is how the story that is centred in some-body's consciousness, passed through a fashioned and constituted mind—not poured straight into the book from the mind of the author, which is a far-away matter, vaguely divined, with no certain edge to it—takes its place as a story dramatically pictured, and as a story, therefore, of stronger stuff than a simple and undramatic report. Thus may be expressed the reason which underlies the novelist's reluctance to *tell* his story and his desire to interpose another presence between himself and the reader. It seems a good reason, good enough to be acted upon more consistently than it is by the masters of the craft. For though their reluctance has had a progressive history, though there are a few principles in the art of fiction that have appeared to emerge and to become established in the course of time, a reader of novels is left at last amazed by the chaos in which the art is still pursued—frankly let it be said. Different schools, debatable theories, principles upheld by some and rejected by others—such disagreement would all be right and natural, it would be the mark of vigour in the art and the criticism of it. But no connected argument, no definition of terms, no formulation of claims, not so much as any ground really cleared and prepared for discussion—what is a novel-reader to make of such a condition and how is he to keep his critical interest alive and alert?

The business of criticism in the matter of fiction seems clear, at any rate. There is nothing more that can usefully be said about a novel until we have fastened upon the question of its making and explored it to some purpose. In all our talk about novels we are hampered and held up by our unfamiliarity with what is called their technical aspect, and that is consequently the aspect to confront. That Jane Austen was an acute observer, that Dickens was a great humourist, that George Eliot had a deep knowledge of provincial character, that our living romancers are so full of life that they are neither to hold nor to bind—we know, we have repeated, we have told each other a thousand times; it is no wonder if attention flags when we hear it all again. It is their books, as well as their talents and attainments, that we aspire to see—their books, which we must recreate for ourselves if we are ever to behold them. And in order to recreate them durably there is the one obvious way—to study the craft, to follow the process, to read constructively. The practice of this method appears to me at this time of day, I confess, the only interest of the criticism of fiction. It seems vain to expect that discourse upon novelists will contain anything new for us until we have really and clearly and accurately seen their books.

And after all it is impossible—that is certain; the book vanishes as we lay hands on it. Every word we say of it, every phrase I have used about a novel in these pages, is loose, approximate, a little more or a little less than the truth. We cannot exactly hit the mark; or if we do, we cannot be sure of it. I do not speak of the just judgement of quality; as for that, any critic of any art is in the same predicament; the value of a picture or a statue is as bodiless as that of a book. But there are times when a critic of literature feels that if only there were one single tangible and measurable fact about a book—if it could be weighed like a statue, say, or measured like a picture—it would be a support in a world of shadows. Such an ingenuous confession, I think it must be admitted, goes to the root of the matter—could we utter our sense of helplessness more candidly? But still among the shadows there is a spark of light that tempts us, there is a hint of the possibility that behind them, beyond them, we may touch a region where the shadows become at least a little more substantial. If that is so, it seems that our chance must lie in the direction I have named. The author of the book was a craftsman, the critic must overtake him at his work and see how the book was made.